Cambridge Elements

Elements in Translation and Interpreting
edited by
Kirsten Malmkjær
University of Leicester

CHARTING TRANSFICTION

Patterns, Open Questions, and Future Directions

Andrea Bergantino
Trinity College Dublin

Shaftesbury Road, Cambridge CB2 8EA, United Kingdom

One Liberty Plaza, 20th Floor, New York, NY 10006, USA

477 Williamstown Road, Port Melbourne, VIC 3207, Australia

314–321, 3rd Floor, Plot 3, Splendor Forum, Jasola District Centre,
New Delhi – 110025, India

Cambridge University Press is part of Cambridge University Press & Assessment, a department of the University of Cambridge.

We share the University's mission to contribute to society through the pursuit of education, learning and research at the highest international levels of excellence.

www.cambridge.org
Information on this title: www.cambridge.org/9781009685467

DOI: 10.1017/9781009685481

© Andrea Bergantino 2026

This publication is in copyright. Subject to statutory exception and to the provisions of relevant collective licensing agreements, no reproduction of any part may take place without the written permission of Cambridge University Press & Assessment.

When citing this work, please include a reference to the DOI 10.1017/9781009685481

First published 2026

A catalogue record for this publication is available from the British Library

ISBN 978-1-009-68546-7 Hardback
ISBN 978-1-009-68544-3 Paperback
ISSN 2633-6480 (online)
ISSN 2633-6472 (print)

Cambridge University Press & Assessment has no responsibility for the persistence or accuracy of URLs for external or third-party internet websites referred to in this publication and does not guarantee that any content on such websites is, or will remain, accurate or appropriate.

For EU product safety concerns, contact us at Calle de José Abascal, 56, 1°, 28003 Madrid, Spain, or email eugpsr@cambridge.org

Charting Transfiction

Patterns, Open Questions, and Future Directions

Elements in Translation and Interpreting

DOI: 10.1017/9781009685481
First published online: January 2026

Andrea Bergantino
Trinity College Dublin
Author for correspondence: Andrea Bergantino, berganta@tcd.ie

Abstract: 'Transfiction' refers to the phenomenon of language mediators portrayed as characters in literature. Research investigating this phenomenon has developed through a long series of case studies. While providing in-depth analyses of different instances of transfiction, case studies have produced findings that are anchored to specific texts, consequently precluding theoretical observations at a higher level of abstraction. Thus, this Element constructs a concentrated profile of transfiction. It asks about the state of the art of this research area and its potential to inform other subfields of translation studies. By adopting a meta-analytical research style, the Element retraces the development of transfiction studies, identifying patterns and lacunae. It then goes on to thread transfiction together with previously disconnected research strands, such as translator studies, suggesting new research questions and methodologies. Ultimately, *Charting Transfiction* provides a reference point for future research in this area, as well as other subfields of translation studies.

Keywords: transfiction, fictional representations, meta-analysis, translator studies, translation studies research practices

© Andrea Bergantino 2026

ISBNs: 9781009685467 (HB), 9781009685443 (PB), 9781009685481 (OC)
ISSNs: 2633-6480 (online), 2633-6472 (print)

Contents

1 Introduction — 1

2 Transfiction Research: The Bigger Picture — 12

3 New Research Avenues — 35

4 What Translators Have to Say — 42

5 Conclusion — 53

References — 56

1 Introduction

In her novel *The Extinction of Irena Rey* (2024), translator and author Jennifer Croft stages a group of eight translators, each named after the language they translate into, gathering reverentially around and working in close collaboration with their author, titular Irena Rey. The plot takes an unexpected turn when Irena disappears, and is found to be writing *The Translators*, a novel within the novel about the translator-protagonists of Croft's story, based on confidential information collected without their consent.

Much like the first few lines of this Element, examples of stories where translators and interpreters are featured as characters, or forms of language mediation become a theme, are often used anecdotally as a curious coincidence to introduce disparate subjects in academic literature, within and outside Translation Studies. John Keats's poem 'On First Looking into Chapman's Homer' prompts discussions on the pressure exerted by past poetic models (Lowe 2015); scenes from Marcel Proust's *In Search of Lost Time* are used as an example of how certain translations come to be seen as classics superior to new retranslations of the same source (Bandia, Hadley, and McElduff 2025, 1–2); and peculiar forms of animalist activism in Olga Tokarczuk's *Drive Your Plow Over the Bones of the Dead* are mentioned to introduce complex concepts, such as eco-translation (Cronin 2023, 8–9).

Although they may not be immediately identifiable, since they are not marketed as a distinct literary genre, narratives pivoting on translator figures or thematising language mediation abound. The ways in which they have been referred to in academic literature have varied in time, ranging from descriptive phrases, such as 'translator fictions' (Thiem 1995, 213), 'fictional representations' (Delabastita and Grutman 2005), and 'racconti di traduzione' [stories of translation] (Lavieri 2007/2016), to more condensed and creative solutions, such as 'transmesis' (Beebee 2012) and 'Übersetzungsfiktionen' [translation fictions] (Babel 2015). They are denoted here as 'transfiction', a portmanteau word coined by Kaindl and Spitzl (2014) which joins 'translation' and 'fiction' together, and has been the term most frequently used for this phenomenon in recent publications (e.g., Miletich 2024b; Spitzer and Oliveira 2023). The fictional component in transfiction is broadly conceived as encompassing written narratives, forms of life writing, audiovisuals, electronic literature, and all sorts of creative texts (Kaindl 2018a, 51–52).

Whether a single translation scene is enough for a work of literature to be categorised as transfiction or the entire text has to revolve around a translator-character is open to debate. Ben-Ari (2010, 225) and Wakabayashi (2011, 88), for instance, point out that scenes of translation in their sources were often found in passing. In any case, scenes of translation span across the centuries as they do across different literary traditions and continents, ranging from classics such as *Don Quixote* and Jorge Luis Borges's short stories (1939/1998) to the work of contemporary authors like Rebecca Kuang (2022), Haruki Murakami (2015), and Elena Ferrante (2013, 2014). Translation scenes, however, are not a prerogative of written narratives. They are also found in films and sitcoms like *Arrival* (Villeneuve 2016)[1] and *Father Ted* (Lowney 1996),[2] plays, such as Brian Friel's *Translations* (1980/2012), advertisements and online content (Abend-David 2019).

Despite being a centuries-old phenomenon (Kaindl 2014, 4–8), the fictional representations of language mediators started attracting scholarly attention only in the early 2000s (see, e.g., Delabastita 2009; Delabastita and Grutman 2005; Strümper-Krobb 2003). At this point, Pagano (2002, 81) reported the 'fictional turn' in Translation Studies, which had been inaugurated by Else Vieira (1995) seven years before in *ComTextos*, a somewhat obscure journal, which by now appears to be unretrievable.

The academic scrutiny of translation scenes has typically revolved around one or a small group of examples, with case studies populating transfiction research. The case study design, along with its characteristics and the inherent limitations it comes with, prompts the research questions of this Element. *Charting Transfiction* asks:

1) What patterns can be identified in existing transfiction research?
2) How can transfiction research diversify the design and methodologies that have traditionally informed this area of enquiry? And what benefits could this diversification bring?
3) How can transfiction be made useful for neighbouring research subfields of Translation Studies?

Accordingly, the overarching aims of this Element are to provide both the phenomenon and the research area of transfiction with a higher degree of visibility and systematisation than it has achieved to date, as well as inspiring other researchers, not only to consider this phenomenon, but also to investigate it following novel methodological approaches. The ultimate objective of the Element is thus to provide future researchers with a reference point that synthesises the practices of knowledge building employed by existing transfiction studies, while also making a pathway for transferability and opening new research avenues.

---

[1] www.youtube.com/watch?v=m8-H5j538oM (last accessed 31 July 2025)
[2] www.youtube.com/watch?v=Zjpx_Jwu6Mo (last accessed 31 July 2025)

There are both contextual and methodological reasons that make these questions worth asking. Literature that makes use of translation as a motif and translators as characters continues to be published (e.g., Calleja 2023; Croft 2024; Kuang 2022; Milkova 2022; Rossari 2023; Xhoga 2025). This kind of literature has been the object of sustained academic engagement (e.g., Kripper 2023; Miletich 2024b; Spitzer and Oliveira 2023), 'foreground[ing] aspects of literary texts that might otherwise pass unnoticed' (Spitzer 2023, 3). In addition, translators who also write non-translated narratives often fictionalise themselves in different forms of prose (e.g., Bianciardi 1962/2019; Lahiri 2015; NíGhríofa 2020), and this phenomenon prompts further questions on literary translation processes, translators' (self-)perceptions, and Translator Studies. These reasons are accompanied by translation and translators becoming increasingly visible in contexts where they have historically been marginalised, ranging from prestigious literary award ceremonies to dedicated book clubs, social networks and other digital spaces. These factors may have an impact on more or less lay imaginaries of translators and translation, which in turn may inform transfiction. On the methodological level, these questions can be answered by adopting a research design that is more comprehensive than and, hence, transcends the small-scale scope of the case study design.

1.1 Methodology

Recent publications (Kripper 2023; Miletich 2024b; Spitzer and Oliveira 2023) show that, in contrast to what Ben-Ari (2014, 122) concluded, the fictional turn has not 'exhausted itself'. However, this turn has developed in close dependence on relatively isolated cases. This tendency has arguably kept fictional enquiry in translation from having a considerable impact on Translation Studies as a whole in terms of how research is carried out, as opposed to the materials researchers can act on. In 2014, when the term 'transfiction' appeared, Ben-Ari asked rhetorically '[h]ow many more novels about frustrated translators/interpreters? Past parody, what remains is tedious repetition' (ibid.). More than ten years later, the same repetition is still apparent, but in the form that most transfiction research has taken, rather than in creative work featuring translators. In her review of Cleary's *The Translator's Visibility* (2021), Strümper-Krobb (2022, 345) notes how 'Cleary's observations about the way in which the theme of translation is mobilized' in Latin American literature 'echo what has been argued by scholars like Klaus Kaindl, Dirk Delabastita and Rosemary Arrojo with regard to texts from a wide range of literatures'. Strümper-Krobb's comments on Cleary's monograph are far from diminishing its contribution to knowledge and, in fact, point to the transferability of existing findings. At the same time, however, these comments may be taken as indicative of a certain repetition in how transfiction research has been designed (see also Bergantino 2024, 237). One way of advancing research in this field in a more systematic and productive way, therefore, is to map how knowledge has been produced in transfiction studies, as opposed to focusing on specific instances of the phenomenon. Meta-research would provide a comprehensive picture of transfiction studies that concentrated engagement with individual texts could not.

While meta-research – or research on research – has gained traction across a variety of scientific domains (Hoon 2013, 526; Ioannidis 2024, 2; Timulak and Creaner 2022, 555), Translation Studies does not appear to follow suit.[3] As observed by Du and Salaets (2025, 2), in their meta-study of collaborative learning in translation and interpreting, in Translation and Interpreting Studies, 'there has been a lack of efforts to synthesise existing literature, including methodological approaches, empirical findings, and limitations, and to explore their implications for future research'. This state of affairs also applies to transfiction research, which has relied heavily, if not exclusively, on case studies and qualitative methods, without necessarily bringing existing studies into conversation. Therefore, to reach the aims outlined earlier, *Charting Transfiction* adopts a meta-analytical research style. In other words, it does not provide another in-depth analysis of one or multiple primary sources that happen to have a transfictional component. Instead, it collates existing studies to capture the state of the art of transfiction research as a whole. To reach this aim, it catalogues the practices of this area of enquiry, namely 'the research methods and procedures used to conduct the research activities' (Causadias et al. 2023, 88), as well as the materials underpinning these activities and the related dissemination strategies. This way, gaps in existing research are found, and new research avenues are identified that could be experimented with in future transfiction studies to bridge these gaps.

Case studies are a common research design in Translation Studies in general (Borg 2023, 35; Hadley 2023, 12; Susam-Sarajeva 2009, 37). Yet literature focusing on their use in translation research specifically is not particularly rich. Case studies have been shown to be an applicable approach to 'illustrat[e] and problematis[e] findings' (Hadley 2023, 10), as well as generating hypotheses (Saldanha and O'Brien 2013, 209). However, as noted in other Translation

---

[3] Meta-research abounds, for instance, in health sciences, while large-scale research designs in Translation Studies beyond literature reviews and corpus-based studies appear to take the form of bibliometric and bibliographic studies (e.g., Huang and Liu 2019; López and Rodríguez 2021; Olalla-Soler, Aixelá, and Rovira-Esteva 2022; Rovira-Esteva, Aixelá, and Olalla-Soler 2019).

Studies subfields like indirect translation, this research style 'may not be the likely means by which the topic comes to be fully integrated within Translation Studies to the extent that its methods and findings inspire research in other topics' (Hadley 2023, 10). Further complications are given by the different understandings of what counts as a case, and whether cases are to be taken as a specific method, a general methodology, or a flexible research style, as well as what each of these alternatives is supposed to look like. In addition, the extent to which the context-bound findings of individual case studies can be generalised is controversial (Flyvbjerg 2006, 226–228; Saldanha and O'Brien 2013, 209; Susam-Sarajeva 2009, 44).

In this context, case studies are understood as 'a particular design of research, where the focus is on an in-depth study of one or a limited number of cases' in the context of which 'particular methods may then be adopted' (Tight 2017, 6, 21). Saldanha and O'Brien (2013, 207) explain that in Translation Studies 'a case can be anything from an individual person (translator, interpreter, author) or text . . ., to a whole organization, such as a training institution or a translation agency, and even a literary system'. In transfiction research, these options have been restricted to texts that contain a transfictional element.

1.1.1 Bibliographic Search, Inclusion, and Exclusion Criteria

The phenomenon that here is referred to as 'transfiction' has been labelled in a variety of ways – or has not been mentioned at all – over the last thirty years, as pointed out earlier. This variety of labels can be subsumed under the 'terminological inflation' observed by Gambier (2023, 319) in Translation Studies more generally. It also has practical consequences for conducting a meta-study, bedevilling the search for appropriate primary sources. First, no single term (e.g., 'transmesis') or string (e.g., 'fictional representations') can be used in isolation to identify all transfiction-related publications. Second, opting for a specific term may lead to results that are not necessarily relevant to the study. 'Transfiction' and its permutations, for instance, are also used in connection to fiction authored by trans writers and to phenomena pertaining to Transmedia Studies (Miletich 2024a, xv). 'Transmesis', instead, encapsulates several phenomena that go beyond and/or are not necessarily connected with the fictional representations of translators as characters, such as code-switching and pseudotranslation (Beebee 2012, 6). Thus, the starting point for the bibliographic search underpinning this meta-study is the literature review of the recent PhD thesis on transfiction, *Translators in Fabula, Bridging Transfiction and Translator Studies through a Comparative Analysis of Contemporary Italian Narratives* (Bergantino 2024). Although anchored to the Italian context, this thesis takes stock of transfiction research and its development in general, identifying its main publication spaces and terminological developments, including special issues of specific journals, monographs, edited collections, and book chapters. While not all items in a certain publication venue mentioned in the thesis may be relevant to the thesis itself, each publication venue identified in the thesis and all its related items have been considered for this meta-analysis to ensure a high level of systematisation and exhaustiveness. For example, while not all articles belonging to a given special issue are reviewed in the thesis, that same special issue was searched for this meta-analysis. Although this approach does not rely on systematically searching online databases, it ensures that all publications captured are relevant to transfiction research, reducing the risk of false positives. It also excludes research outputs that use 'transfiction' to refer to different topics and phenomena or happen to cite publications that include this word in their bibliography or in the researcher's biographical note, while bearing no or very little relevance to the publication itself.

The language of publication has been restricted to English in the attempt to strike a balance between personal limitations and linguistic equity. Why include publications in English, German, and Italian – the languages I happen to speak – but not those in Portuguese, Spanish, and Turkish, of which I have partial understanding or no command at all? The choice of English also ensures that most recent publications in transfiction, which have appeared in this language, are included.[4] It has to be acknowledged that transfiction publications in other languages, especially German, are highly represented – in fact, foundational – in transfiction research (e.g., Babel 2015; Kaindl and Kurz 2010b; Kaindl and Kurz 2008, 2005; Strümper-Krobb 2009; Wilhelm 2010). Despite possibly different rhetorical traditions in academic writing, however, research designs, methods, and primary sources used in non-English publications might not differ substantially from those used in English-language publications.

Another criterion for inclusion and exclusion is of a thematic nature. While transfiction is understood in this context as creative texts featuring language mediators, academic scrutiny of translation fictions has actively tried to stretch the borders of this definition to encompass other phenomena, such as pseudotranslation and self-translation (Ben-Ari and Levin 2016; Woodsworth 2018). For this study, these two phenomena are not automatically considered to be transfiction, unless existing studies have engaged with a narrative that stages a pseudotranslator or a self-translator as a character.

---

[4] For language distribution in Translation Studies research and the dominance of English in this context, see Olalla-Soler, Aixelá, and Rovira-Esteva (2022, 25–27).

1.1.2 Corpus and Categories of Analysis

Keeping these criteria in mind, a total of 113 publications were found and listed in a spreadsheet, so as to create a structured, tabular dataset, and consequently conduct a descriptive analysis of it, as well as visualising its patterns by means of charts and tables (see McDonough Dolmaya 2024, 143–146). The bibliographic search gathered publications from 1995 to 2025, thus covering the last thirty years. To answer the first two research questions of this Element, each publication was read with a view to identifying features that were then grouped into predetermined categories. These categories are 'author', 'year of publication', 'type of publication', 'research design', 'methodology', 'statement of purpose', 'materials', 'key words', and 'authors of primary sources'. While author details are easily found in the title page of each publication, information pertaining to the other categories of analysis was retrieved from the abstracts and the introduction section of each publication. This choice is due to these two spaces being expected to contain and describe essential components of a research output, such as methodologies and primary sources. After this first categorisation process, more categories were established a posteriori in relation to research design and methodologies, specifically, based on observable patterns emerging from the first phase.

1.2 The Fictional Turn: An Overview

While analyses of individual literary texts in transfiction research abound, the number of comprehensive overviews of this subfield is quite modest. Publications providing a reference point in the field might be expected to be found in encyclopaedias and handbooks, along with introduction chapters. The corpus of this study includes only two encyclopaedia entries, two handbook chapters, and seven publications with the function of introducing edited collections and special issues. Collectively, these are 11 publications out of 113, constituting 12.4% of the corpus. This section synthesises this subgroup of publications, together with other landmark publications, to provide an overview of the recurrent themes, functions, and types of narratives that fictional translators have been found to appear with, contextualising them within the fictional turn in Translation Studies.

The fictional turn has relied on two overarching principles, one of a theoretical nature and the other of a methodological one. The first principle is condensed by Pagano (2002, 80–81) in the argument that 'fictional works contain a theoretical component' and, hence, fiction can be incorporated in Translation Studies 'as a medium of theoretical speculation' and 'translation theorization'. This idea of fiction being complementary to traditional academic research has been reiterated by several transfiction scholars, becoming a recurrent justification for research engaging with fictional representations despite conspicuous terminological diversity (e.g., Arrojo 2014; Gentzler 2008; Lavieri 2007/2016; Spitzer 2023; Spitzl 2014). The fictional turn does not operate under the illusion of using fiction as a source of evidence or crystallised factual information on translation theory and practice. Giraldo and Piracón (2023, 112) remain cognisant of this logical complication when they explain that

> the connections we establish between fiction and theory are always contingent, constructed by readers, so we will not be appealing to a notion of an idealized, accessible intention in which authors may have purposefully been articulating their own works using the key of an outside theory, or even to the possibility that they may have been at all interested in offering insights on translation or translators.

Fiction does not necessarily overlap or aim to reproduce reality (John 2016, 36; Kaindl 2023, 25; 2018b, 164). Thus, rather than proposing 'a complete postmodern fictionalization of the world', transfiction is used as a basis to reflect on 'points of intersection' between fiction and reality, 'points that can contribute to a fruitful exchange and the discovery of new ideas' (Kaindl 2018b, 159). The fictional turn harnesses the potential of fictional representations to offer 'a comment on the socio-cultural values and the state of the world we live in' (Delabastita and Grutman 2005, 24), a point raised about fictional characters more generally (Carroll 2016, 84; John 2016, 46; Schoeneborn and Cornelissen 2022, 140, 152). Fictional representations of translators, in particular, are argued to provide a 'mimetic treatment' of 'those 'black-box' aspects of the translational process that translations as finished products obscure' (Beebee 2012, 3), such as affective elements (Anderson 2005, 181). Moreover, they have been used to deconstruct clichés traditionally associated with translation and translators, including the nebulous notions of 'original', 'equivalence', 'fidelity', 'authorship', along with their related dichotomies (Arrojo 2018, 18; Kaindl 2018b, 161; Lavieri 2007/2016, 63–82).

While theorisation based on fictional representations has been widely justified, the ways in which this can happen in practice have not been outlined in great detail. Hagedorn (2006, 11) was probably one of the first scholars to provide a broad description of how research on the theme of translation can be done. Hagedorn identified an underlying methodological principle in the 'inversión de la perspectiva traductológica' [inversion of the translational perspective]. Accordingly, this kind of research is not concerned with finding out what happens when a text is translated into another language and the related strategies adopted by the translator, but with how writers represent translators and translation in their narratives, and what characteristics and implications these representations may have (see also Wilson 2007, 382).

Scholarly engagement with 'the triad fiction-theory-translation', as Pagano (2002, 81) puts it, has resulted in the identification of thematic constellations, recurrent functions of translations as a narrative element, and points at which fiction and academic enquiry can meet. Delabastita and Grutman list possible themes accompanying the fictional representations of multilingualism and translators, namely *trust, loyalty versus betrayal, invisibility and authorial ambition, untranslatability, trauma,* and *identity* (2005, 23; emphasis in the original). Because it is often used metaphorically, as opposed to an act of linguistic transfer, translation can also be used because of its 'expressive, symbolic, and representative potential ... to address themes of *movement*, such as *migration, flight, displacement, wandering, restlessness*, or *uprooting*' – in sum, 'a whole plethora of *transfer processes*' (Kaindl 2014, 2, 4; emphasis added). Many of these topics, by now, have become recurrent talking points both in transfictional texts and academic literature more broadly. Delabastita (2020, 2009) goes on to describe some of the contexts in which fictional language mediators are likely to be encountered. These range from the transmission of divine messages in sacred texts to science fiction, from narratives of conflict, broadly conceived, to those of colonisation and espionage. Ben-Ari (2014, 114–116), instead, proposes a tentative typology of novels with translator-protagonists, identifying four categories: postcolonial novels, poststructural novels, best-sellers that capitalise on translation as a fashionable theme, and novels that parody the same theme and/or genre.

Moving on from the themes to the roles performed by translation as a narrative element, Kaindl (2012, 146–147) identifies five main functions:

1. The *figure-characterizing function* assigns certain characteristics to fictional language mediators, which often take the form of translatorial clichés, such as betrayers, uprooted subjects, and facilitators. Associated with this function is the hypothesis that transfiction may be taken as indicative of how specific cultures think of translators and interpreters, a hypothesis which builds on 'Lévi-Strauss' (1985, 9) thesis that societies frequently ascribe certain traits to certain professions' (Kaindl 2014, 17).
2. When the topic of translation works as an allusion to wider philosophical matters and societal and historical concerns it performs a *symbolic function*.
3. Similarly, the *metaphorical function* shifts translation from a text-based act to a metaphor, such as cultural translation.
4. The *meta-narrative function* occurs when the entire narrative hinges on the theme of language mediation itself. Kaindl (2012, 147) notes elsewhere that

this function is privileged by authors who are also translators and use fiction as a site to reflect on their profession.
5. The *meta-fictional function* occurs when translation is used as a narrative device conducive to the unfolding of the plot, typically in the form of mysterious manuscripts and their (pseudo)translation. This function overlaps with those described by Hagedorn (2006) in his anatomy of fictitious translations, as well as those traditionally ascribed to pseudotranslation, such as the introduction of stylistic novelties, mechanisms to deflect authorship, as well as the responsibility it comes with, and parody (Bergantino 2023; Kupsch-Losereit 2014; Maher 2019; Rath 2024; Strümper-Krobb 2018).

While the identification of these themes and functions offers reference points for transfiction research, it does not deal with the complications arising from the fact that the ways in which fiction and academic literature describe the world are, by definition, distinct. In the context of the fictional turn, this discrepancy is perceived as an advantage for research. Pagano (2002, 97), for instance, explains that 'fiction represents a genre that informs translation thinking from a comprehensive perspective, sensitive to relationships and movements difficult to capture through more orthodox analyses that do not consider fictional texts'. What these relationships and movements might look like and what implications they may have for translation theory-building and hypotheses, however, is often left to interpretation and philosophical observations. An attempt at pinpointing these relationships between (trans)fiction and academic enquiry is presented in a chapter of *A History of Modern Translation Knowledge*, where Kaindl (2018a, 53–54) lists four points of intersections:

1. The first point is *theory*. Fictional representations are seen as a potential starting point to develop theoretical understandings of translation, thematising concerns that are resonant with academic issues, such as the relationship between translations and their sources, authorship and translatorship, in a way that is often reminiscent of translation theories originating in deconstructive and postmodern approaches.
2. *Identity* follows, being thematised in transfiction in a variety of ways, ranging from the individual to the national level, while also considering migration and translingual and transcultural identities.
3. *Poetics* is the third intersection. Reference is made here to Lavieri's *Translatio in Fabula* (2007/2016), where it is argued that '[l]a valorizzazione del traduttore e del suo lavoro diventano possibili soltanto attraverso il riconoscimento di una poetica che gli sia propria' [the valorisation of translators and their work becomes possible only through the acknowledgement of their own poetics] (Lavieri 2007/2016, 51).

4. *Pedagogy* refers to 'the potential of fictional texts for translator and interpreter training' (Kaindl 2018a, 54). Cronin (2009, xi) had already encouraged the pedagogical use of transfictional materials, pointing to films featuring language mediation as valid teaching and learning resources. Recent pedagogical applications of transfiction are found in Cleary (2021) and Kripper (2023).

In 'The Remaking of the Translator's Reality. The Role of Fiction in Translation Studies', Kaindl (2018b, 162–168) extends this list of intersections, adding historiography and anthropology to theory, identity, poetics, and pedagogy. These intersections are presented here in light of 'the epistemological knowledge that can be gained from fictional representations of translators and interpreters' (ibid., 158).

5. *Historiography*, like fiction, is seen as far from providing bare facts because 'the depiction of historical events inevitably involves narrative emplotments' (Kaindl 2018a, 163). This connection between fiction and historiography is also teased out by Spitzer (2017, 15), who explains that when 'narrating events from a distant past, ... a fictionality resounds from the very possibility of writing such a narrative with direct speech and an interiority assigned to characters'. A famous example is the story of Doña Marina, also known as la Malinche, the interpreter of Hernán Cortés who is often invoked in transfiction research (e.g., Cleary 2021; Gentzler 2008; Valdeón 2011).
6. Finally, Kaindl (2018b, 164–168) argues that fictional representations intersect with *anthropology* because authors of transfiction draw from a society's imagery of translation as a context-bound phenomenon. Fictional representations, therefore, are 'rooted in a *collective translatorial memory* of a society' (ibid., 165; emphasis in the original). Accordingly, analysing transfiction would imply dealing with the conceptualisations of translation proper to specific cultures and traditions in space and time.

The findings of existing transfiction research presented in this section, in terms of themes transfiction has been found to appear with, the types of novels featuring translator-characters, the functions of translation within fiction, and the intersections of (trans)fiction and other fields of academic enquiry are summarised in Table 1.

Identifying these themes, functions, and intersections in conjunction with transfiction as a phenomenon and a research area is conducive to a better mapping of transfiction and transfiction research, which have both been largely unsystematised. Existing literature does not suggest that these functions and

Table 1 Themes, functions, intersections, and types of novels

Themes	Functions	Intersections	Types of novels
loyalty vs betrayal	figure-characterising	theory	postcolonial
(in)visibility	symbolic	identity	post-structural
authorial ambition	metaphorical	poetics	best-sellers
untranslatability	meta-narrative	pedagogy	parodies
trauma	meta-fictional	historiography	
identity		anthropology	
colonisation			
diplomacy and espionage			
movement and transfer			

intersections are in a relation of mutual exclusion. The difference between symbolic function and metaphorical function, for instance, is very nuanced. Likewise, historical narratives about translator figures in a specific context may feed not only into historiography, but also anthropology and pedagogy. Kripper (2023, 43) exemplifies this possibility, anchoring her area-specific analysis of Latin American transfiction to a culture of 'mistranslation and other digressive approaches [that] disrupt official historical discourses in contrapuntal narratives that reread and rewrite history'. In addition, Kripper (2023) uses her case studies of transfiction for pedagogical purposes, proposing questions for class discussion at the end of each chapter of her monograph. Therefore, while this categorisation represents a valid reference point when navigating transfiction and its publishing landscape, it may well be the case that the fabric of functions, intersections, and themes of transfiction is much more fine-spun than it appears here.

2 Transfiction Research: The Bigger Picture

2.1 Themes in Transfiction and Transfiction Research

When it comes to themes, in particular, the identification of clear-cut thematic areas can be far from straightforward within and outside transfiction research, for several reasons. First, subjective interpretations of a narrative can easily result in somewhat arbitrary thematic categories. Second, themes themselves are often hard to tell apart, so matters of identity could be closely bound up with the phenomenon of self-translation, and the act of writing could be perceived as encapsulating that of translating, as opposed to the two being completely different processes. Similarly, the idea of transfer can play out on a linguistic level, as well as on an existential or physical one. Third, methodological complications can influence this identification. Hadley (2023, 13) notes that '[p]articularly for topics that could be seen as contentious, it may be especially problematic to rely on forms of analysis that do not have any obvious means of accounting and control for confirmation bias, such as close reading'. Even when conducting a meta-analytical study, nevertheless, it is complicated to tell apart the themes found in each publication from the themes of their respective primary sources, especially because this research design zooms out to a wide, comprehensive view of existing research, as opposed to offering a detailed review of each item in the dataset.

To provide a thematic overview trying to curb subjective interpretivism, while also accounting for more than a hundred publications, key words were extracted from each publication whenever available, being taken as indicative of the main themes with which the publications engage. When no key word was indicated explicitly, words appearing in section titles were used. These were filtered further to identify those key words and the related themes that appear with the highest frequency in the dataset. Further filtering was applied to those concepts that tend to appear in pairs, typically with one concept being the counterpart of or closely related to the other, such as 'invisibility' and 'visibility' or 'infidelity' and 'fidelity', as well as 'colonialism' and 'postcolonialism'. The results of these procedures are illustrated in Figure 1.

'Identity' was found to be the most represented topic in the corpus (14.8%), followed by '(in)visibility' (13%), research dealing explicitly with 'interpreters' (9.3%), rather than translators in general, '(in)fidelity' (7.4%), and

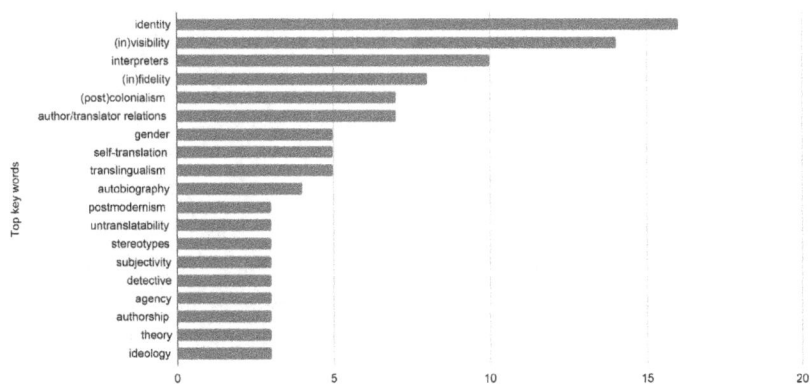

Figure 1 Top key words

'(post)colonialism' (6.5%) at the same place as 'author/translator relations' (also 6.5%). 'Gender', 'self-translation', and 'translingualism' follow, sharing the same frequency (4.6%). 'Autobiography' is represented in 3.7% of the corpus. Other topics ranging from 'postmodernism' to 'ideology' appear less frequently, with each accounting for 2.8% of the corpus.

Figure 1 confirms identity as one of the underlying topics in transfiction research. Identity stands out as a multifaceted and complex concept, as it can refer to single individuals or groups, as well as nations and even larger geographical areas and cultural traditions (Cronin 2000; Gentzler 2008; Godbout 2014), spanning postcolonial and migratory configurations (Polezzi 2012, 354) and globalisation (Cronin 2003, 73; Kaindl 2012, 145). The increase in the number of narratives featuring fictional translators, in fact, has often been traced back to globalisation and the challenges it has posed for individuals, translation, and society in general (Delabastita 2009; Kaindl 2016; Kaindl and Kurz 2010a; Strümper-Krobb 2003).

Other high-frequency themes shown in Figure 1 have been the subject of ongoing debate not only in transfiction research, but in Translation Studies more broadly. Invisibility epitomises this pattern, being 'one of the most ubiquitous concepts in contemporary translation studies' (Freeth 2024, 7). Much research in transfiction has engaged with this topic to argue that fictional representations may contribute to elevating translators from their notorious state of invisibility. This pattern in transfiction research, which has been labelled as 'compensation theory' (Bergantino 2024, 118-119), emerges from studies on both transfiction in general and individual cases (Beebee 2012, 217; Cronin 2009, x–xi; Kaindl 2014, 4; Kripper 2023, 111; Strümper-Krobb 2009, 14–21; Wilhelm 2010, 88–93; Wilson 2007, 381–382). To date, there has been little challenge to this theory of augmented translator visibility through fictional representation (Ben-Ari 2021, 159; 2014, 122; 2010, 235–236).

Likewise, the notion of (in)fidelity is by now a cliché in translation theory, in close connection to the idea of equivalence. The myth of translation as a sameness-driven practice has been dispelled as one of 'the innumerable fictions' in Translation Studies (Kaindl 2018b, 161), an 'untruth' (Cronin 2000, 109). Lavieri (2007/2016, 67–69) counts equivalence, faithfulness, and literality among common misconceptions of translating, and Venuti (2019, ix) explicitly traces the qualifier 'faithful' back to 'the simplistic, clichéd thinking that has limited our understanding of it [translation] for millennia'. The fact that much effort has been put into demonstrating the fallacies on which the narrative of translation as simplistic replication is based is significant. It indirectly shows that the assumption under which translators operate is often that of translation conceived not as a transformative endeavour, but as an unvaried replication of its sources. The '*equivalence supermeme*', in Chesterman's words, 'has continued to flourish' (2016, 14; emphasis in the original). This might indicate that the nebulous notion of 'equivalence' – and the expectations it comes with – is still a deeply rooted idea in the lay imagery of translation, which may subsequently percolate through fiction.

A common thread between these three topics is that, while attracting notable scholarly attention, they are not particularly well-defined and/or accompanied by detailed, interoperable descriptions. Consequently, they might appeal to both transfiction researchers and researchers in other areas of specialisation within Translation Studies precisely because they are flexible concepts, lending themselves to a variety of understandings. (In)fidelity, for example, has been used in connection to gendered roles in writing and translating (Arrojo 2018, 133; Wilson 2009, 189), as well as being taken as a purposefully deviating strategy of mistranslation (Kripper 2023, 6–7).

2.2 Transfiction Research in Time

The distribution of English-language publications in transfiction research in the time frame 1995–2025 is shown in Figure 2. The figure illustrates the development of this research line, which moved from scattered publications between 1995 and 2004 to a notable peak in 2005, followed by the highest concentration of publications in 2014. This number then drops considerably, to rise again more recently, between 2023 and 2024. The evolution of transfiction research in time captured in the figure is far from being gradual. The number of

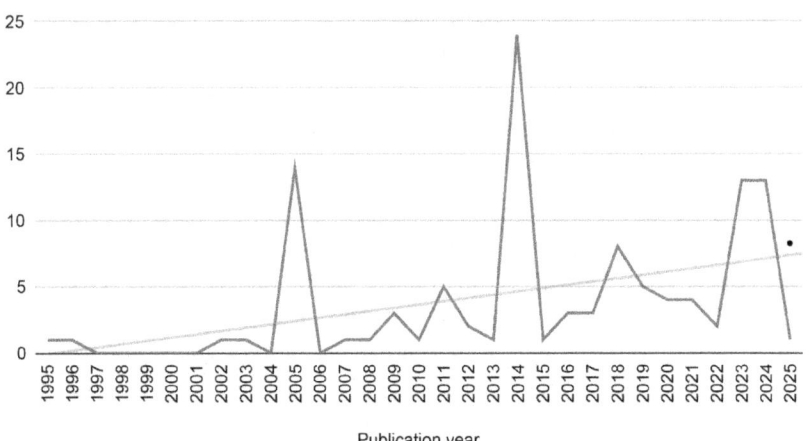

Figure 2 Distribution of transfiction publications in time

publications does not increase steadily. Instead, three main upward trends can be noticed, accompanied by periods of relatively little growth.

These trends are found in connection with 2005 (fourteen publications, equal to 12.4% of the corpus), 2014 (twenty-four publications, equal to 21.2% of the corpus), and 2023–2024 (thirteen publications each, and each equal to 11.5% of the corpus). Another increase can be seen in 2018 (eight publications, equal to 7.1% of the corpus). These peaks correspond to the years in which landmark studies in transfiction research were published.

The first attempt at systematically exploring what would later be called 'transfiction' was the fourth volume of *Linguistica Antverpiensia* edited by Delabastita and Grutman (2005) under the title 'Fictionalising Translation and Multilingualism'. This volume focused on 'the two possible outcomes of language contact', namely multilingualism and translation (Delabastita and Grutman 2005, 12), as opposed to considering the representations of translator-characters as a distinct phenomenon. At this stage, therefore, transfiction was conflated with the 'fictional representations' of both topics (ibid., 14). This special issue, which challenged strict disciplinary boundaries to embrace linguistics, history, and sociology, arguably resulted in enhanced visibility of fictional translators as a phenomenon worth exploring, as well as in enhanced systematisation. The general and descriptive terminology used by Delabastita and Grutman was then also used in other book chapters and articles (e.g., Kaindl 2018a, 2016; Wakabayashi 2011). It is significant that the first time the *Routledge Encyclopedia of Translation Studies* included an entry dedicated to fictional representations was in 2009, four years after the 2005 thematic issue of *Linguistica Antverpiensia*, reiterated in its latest edition (Delabastita 2009, 2020).

Acknowledging the work of Delabastita and Grutman, Cronin drew attention 'to translators not so much as agents of representation but as objects of representation' in films (Cronin 2009, x). Beebee's notion of 'transmesis' followed (2012), and it arguably contributed to consolidating this subfield, straddling Translation Studies and Literary Studies. 'Transmesis', nevertheless, does not refer precisely or solely to the representation of translators in fiction. Instead, it denotes 'the mimesis of the interrelated phenomena of translation, multilingualism, and code-switching' (Beebee 2012, 6). The collection *Transfiction: Research into the Realities of Translation Fiction*, edited by Kaindl and Spitzl (2014), was published two years later. In its introduction chapter, Kaindl (2014, 4) contextualises the phenomenon of transfiction, as well as providing its definition along with a description of the collection's scope:

> [o]n its journey through different contexts and uses, translation now has become a central motif and topic of the narrative arts, of literature and film.

> This development is doubtlessly rooted in the mobility of the concept, its changeability and its many layers of meaning. Thus, this present volume focusses on transfiction, i.e. the introduction and (increased) use of translation-related phenomena in fiction. It investigates what this development means for translation studies, what theoretical and methodological issues it raises, and how we might respond to them.

Since then, the term transfiction has been used regularly to denote the phenomenon under discussion, becoming entrenched in academic usage via international conferences and the publications originating from them (Ben-Ari and Levin 2016, 339; Kolb, Pöllabauer, and Kadrić 2024, 12; Kripper 2023, 5; Miletich 2024a, xvii; Woodsworth 2021, 293; Woodsworth and Lane-Mercier 2018, 3). In the same foundational volume, Spitzl (2014, 364–365) summarises Kaindl's definition of transfiction as 'an aestheticized imagination of translatorial action', placing an emphasis on the embodied experience of translation, as opposed to the 'dehumanization of theories and concepts'. It was not until 2014, therefore, that fictional representations of translators and language mediation were taken as research topics not necessarily dependent on or interwoven with forms of multilingualism (cf. Sternberg 1981), and in purely abstract terms.

To date, the highest number of publications in transfiction research occurred in 2014, which is reflective of the edited collection, *Transfiction* (Kaindl and Spitzl 2014) being a designated space for the establishment and dissemination of transfiction research, gathering a total of twenty-four contributions. Other book-length publications followed, with some of them intentionally trying to go beyond transfiction. These publications included contributions on translation phenomena that problematise traditional dichotomies between 'original' and translation, author and translator, and other 'fictions of translation' as opposed to transfiction (Woodsworth and Lane-Mercier 2018, 4). This research trend can be summarised in the following question, asked by Rosenwald (2016, 358): 'What model of the relation between author and translator would we create if we acknowledged from the start that there was no way to distinguish in essence between the two persons, roles, activities, speech acts?'

In 2023 and 2024, where the latest upward trends in the number of publications can be observed, three other book-length publications appeared, a monograph (Kripper 2023) and two edited collections (Miletich 2024b; Spitzer and Oliveira 2023). Rather than continuing to push the boundaries of the definition of transfiction, these publications went back to the idea of fictional representations of translators and translation, while also conceptualising transfiction as an '*approach* to theorizing translation' that 'foregrounds aspects of literary texts that might otherwise pass unnoticed or without sufficient interpretive scrutiny' (Spitzer 2023, 3; emphasis in the original).

As shown in Figure 2, the number of publications drops suddenly in 2025. This sharp drop is likely due to this research being conducted in the same year and the time constraints this implies. It is possible that more transfiction research will be published in 2025, but these publications are not captured here because the data collection phase of this meta-analysis was completed prior to their release. Figure 2 shows a trend line signifying an average calculated based on the count of publications per year, as well as a data point in relation to 2025. This point represents a forecasted value taking into account the trend over the last thirty years and projecting this trend into the future. This projection estimates that the number of transfiction publications in 2025 will be approximately eight, subject to the continuation of current trajectories. Irrespective of exact numbers, the number of publications is expected to drop again, which reinforces the fluctuating pattern observed over the last thirty years.

Collectively, the publications which appeared in conjunction with the peaks illustrated in Figure 2 can be taken as research-defining because they marked a shift in the study of transfiction from a vastly unsystematic, anecdotal, and incidental approach to establishing a subfield with its own specificity. However, it would be simplistic to assume that a higher number of publications is directly connected to the impact or significance of the same publications. Fewer publications may have been published in periods which do not constitute an upward trend in the number of published research outputs, while still being significant for the development of the field. Further hypotheses on this situation can be made based not only on the number of publications, but also on the forms they have taken.

2.3 Types of Publication

Book chapters represent the most frequent type of publication in transfiction research over the last thirty years, as is apparent in Figure 3. The bibliographic search identified fifty-six book chapters, constituting almost half (49.6%) of the publishing landscape in transfiction research. The second most frequent publication type is journal articles: forty-four articles were identified, accounting for 38.9% of the corpus. Four monographs, that is, book-length publications authored by a single researcher, instead, make up 4.4% of the corpus. References like encyclopaedia entries and handbook chapters constitute 3.6% of the corpus, with the same percentage being represented by student work, including master's dissertations and PhD theses. The underrepresentation of student work might depend on its lesser visibility on research engines like Google Scholar than those of research articles, as it is typically stored in

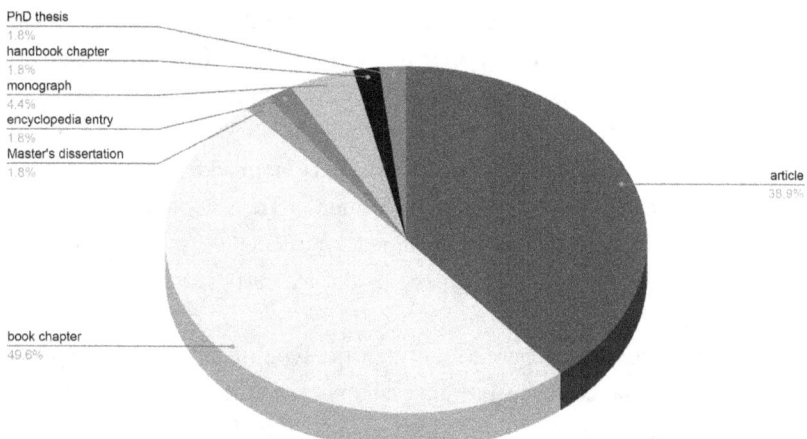

Figure 3 Publication types

institutional repositories. Another reason might be the notably peripheral position of fictional representations in Translation Studies syllabi, which results in students not being exposed to this topic as much as they are to core translation theories. It is indicative, for example, that fictional representations are not dealt with in classic reference points of the Translation Studies class, such as the various editions of *Introducing Translation Studies* (Munday, Pinto, and Blakesley 2022) and *The Translation Studies Reader* (Venuti 2012).

It is noteworthy that Figures 2 and 3 would both look quite different, were German-language publications added to the corpus. These include collections edited by Kaindl and Kurz (Kaindl and Kurz 2010b, 2008, 2005), each gathering between twenty-two and twenty-five chapters authored by different contributors. Adding these publications to the English-language dataset would have a significant impact on the quantification process and the related results, leading to a more homogenous distribution of publications in the five-year period 2005–2010. This addition would also confirm that book chapters are by far the prevailing form of publication in transfiction research. Counting handbook chapters together with the more general category of 'book chapters' would also lead to similar consequences. Including non-English-language work by Hagedorn (2006), Lavieri (2007/2016), Strümper-Krobb (2009), Wilhelm (2010), and Babel (2015), instead, would lead to a higher number of monographs, while confirming the dominance of books over articles.

The fact that book chapters, along with articles, constitute the majority of publications in transfiction research reflects trends in the Translation Studies publishing ecosystem. A discipline-specific analysis conducted on BITRA (the

Bibliography of Interpreting and Translation) reveals that 'journal articles are ... the most numerous research output in TS ... However, books and book chapters together account for 53.6% of the outputs from 1951 up to the present [2019], whereas journal articles account for 46.3% in the same period' (Rovira-Esteva, Aixelá, and Olalla-Soler 2019, 163). In addition, while journal articles are the most frequent type of publication in Translation Studies, 'books and book chapters together are the document types cited the most' (ibid., 168).

The distribution of publication types over the last thirty years is illustrated by Figure 4.

Correlating the year of publication with the type of publication, Figure 4 shows that 2005 and 2014 saw the highest number of articles and book chapters published, respectively. As discussed earlier, a dedicated volume of *Linguistica Antverpiensia* (Delabastita and Grutman 2005) and the edited collection *Transfiction* (Kaindl and Spitzl 2014) appeared in these years. The same pattern can be observed in 2023 and 2024, with two other edited collections being released (Miletich 2024b; Spitzer and Oliveira 2023).

Another observable pattern is that most articles and book chapters tend to appear in clusters. This tendency raises questions about the dissemination dynamics of transfiction research, not only in terms of publication venues, but also on the nature of this research per se. These grouped patterns, whereby the highest concentration of articles and book chapters appear in the same year, might be indicative of some sort of dependence of transfiction research on special occasions, rather than pointing to transfiction being an object of widespread scholarly engagement. The peaks shown in Figure 2 and the distribution

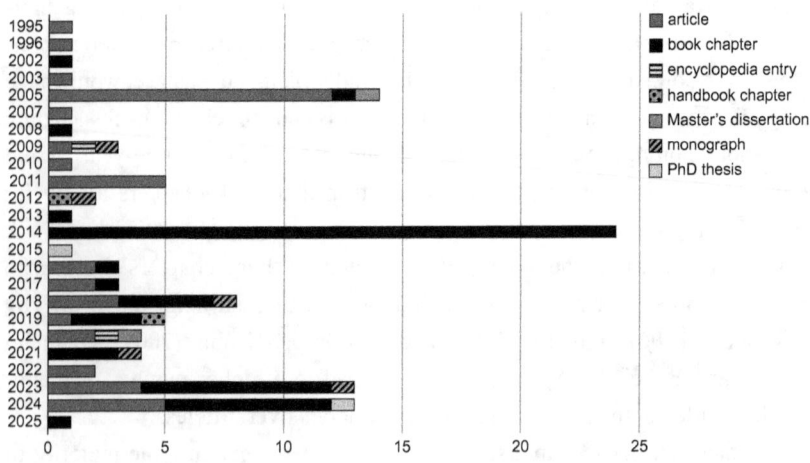

Figure 4 Publication types 1995–2025

of publication types over the last thirty years shown in Figure 4 might suggest that transfiction research depends on variables, such as a journal's special issues, conferences, and calls for chapters. In turn, this supposed dependence might imply that research in the field has been driven by a relatively small group of researchers, as opposed to transfiction being of general interest in the Translation Studies community at large.

There have been at least five conferences either entirely dedicated to transfiction or showcasing transfiction research to a lesser extent, and as many research outputs (edited collections and special issues), which are more or less explicitly related to them (Ben-Ari and Levin 2016, 339; Kolb, Pöllabauer, and Kadrić 2024, 12; Kripper 2023, 5; Miletich 2024a, xvii; Woodsworth 2021, 293; Woodsworth and Lane-Mercier 2018, 3). These are shown in chronological order in Table 2.

While publications resulting from these events do not focus exclusively on transfiction, the concentration of most journal articles and book chapters in this subfield within the three-year period following each of them supports the hypothesis that transfiction research has tended to rely on specific initiatives, rather than being a mainstream area of study. Further evidence for this hypothesis can be drawn from a large-scale thematic analysis of topics recurring with high frequency in Translation Studies in the period 1972–2021, where there is no room for transfiction and/or other terms referring to the same phenomenon (Olalla-Soler, Aixelá, and Rovira-Esteva 2022, 24). Another bibliometric analysis of Translation Studies from 2014 to 2018 reinforces this hypothesis, as transfiction as a phenomenon is not listed among the most frequently explored research topics (Huang and Liu 2019, 41–43).

2.4 Research Designs and Methodologies

Figure 5 leaves little room for interpretation as to what the most frequent research design is in transfiction research, with case studies constituting almost 80% of the corpus. While the 'introduction' (seven publications) and 'conclusion' (one publication) designs are self-explanatory, this may not be the case for the other categories of research designs. So, before discussing the overwhelming majority of case studies, the other three research designs included in the figure are described.

- 'Case studies' (90 publications) of transfiction are understood here as in-depth analyses of one or a small group of literary texts featuring language mediators, in the context of which qualitative methods and philosophical argumentation are typically adopted to substantiate the analysis. Their titles

Table 2 Conferences on transfiction

Title	Year	Host institution	Website	Subsequent publication
First International Conference on Fictional Translators and Interpreters in Literature and Film	2011	University of Vienna	https://transfiction.univie.ac.at/	*Transfiction. Research into the Realities of Translation Fiction* (Kaindl and Spitzl 2014)
Beyond Transfiction: Translators and (Their) Authors	2013	Tel-Aviv University	https://humanities1.tau.ac.il/tirgum_eng/index.php/component/article/5144-main/33-welcome	*Translators and (Their) Authors in the Fictional Turn* (Ben-Ari and Levin 2016)
Transfiction 3: The Fictions of Translation	2015	Concordia University	www.concordia.ca/events/conferences/transfiction.html	*The Fictions of Translation* (Woodsworth 2018)
Staging the Literary Translator. Roles, Identities, Personalities	2018	University of Vienna	https://translit2018.univie.ac.at/home/	*Literary Translator Studies* (Kaindl, Kolb, and Schlager 2021)
Transfiction: The Fictional Eye of Translation Studies (NeMLA)	2022	Tufts University and University of Buffalo	https://call-for-papers.sas.upenn.edu/cfp/2021/07/19/transfiction-the-fictional-eye-of-translation-studies-nemla-2022	*Transfiction: Characters in Search of Translation Studies* (Miletich 2024b)

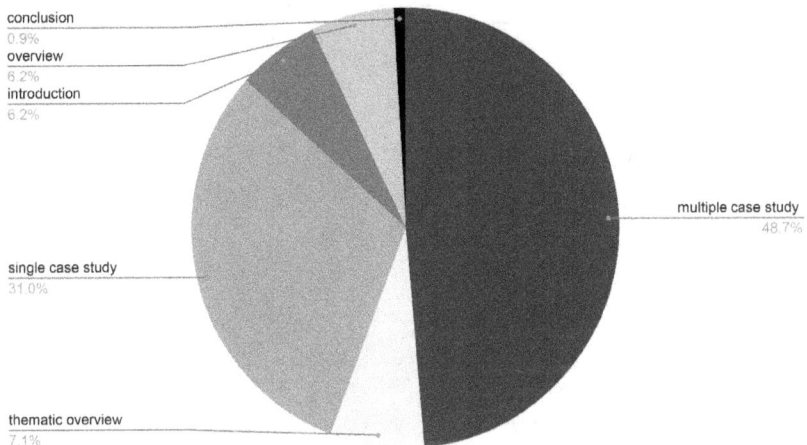

Figure 5 Research designs

tend to follow formulaic patterns, which can be summarised as 'phenomenon being considered' + 'in' + 'name of author(s)' + 'titles of primary sources' or 'qualifier + fiction'.
- Much like 'introductions', the category 'overviews' (seven publications) refers mostly to reference publications, such as handbook chapters and encyclopaedia entries, which offer a digest and background information in terms of chronological developments and main topics within the subfield, with the function of contextualising transfiction as a phenomenon and object of enquiry. Unlike 'introductions', they do not introduce edited collections or a journal's special issue.
- 'Thematic overviews' (eight publications) differ from general 'overviews' in that they do not aim to outline the different connotations of transfiction as a general phenomenon or the history of its development. Instead, they outline and discuss a number of topics emerging from their primary sources, without producing a concentrated analysis of any of them, specifically. This concentrated analysis, instead, is what characterises case studies.

Another design emerging from the corpus is represented by a subgroup of twenty-one 'area-specific studies', in the context of which a case can be represented both by literary texts and/or the areas being explored. These studies embed their primary sources into a wider geographical region, contextualising these texts in the culture and literary tradition of this area, instead of selecting sources across diverse contexts based on their thematic analogies. A breakdown of these studies is provided by Figure 6, where the percentages refer to

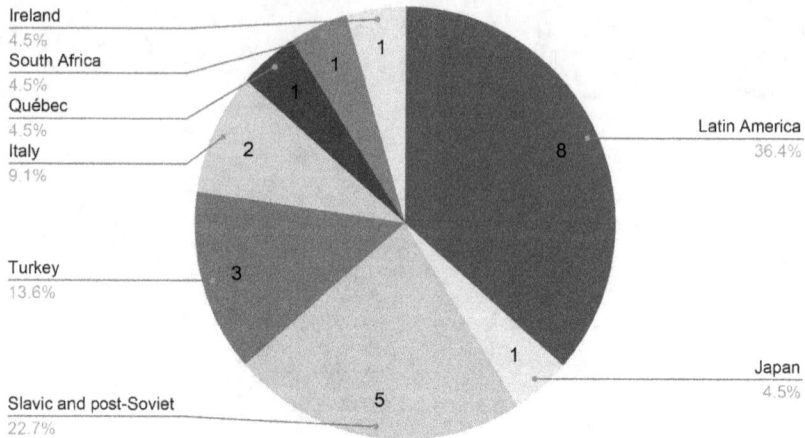

Figure 6 Area-specific studies

this subgroup of twenty-one publications, as opposed to the entire corpus. Publications were assigned to this subgroup not solely based on the country or language of origin of the author of the primary sources being examined, or on the setting of these sources. This choice would have led to all publications being somehow specific to a certain area. Instead, area-specific studies were grouped together based on the researcher's explicit aim to investigate transfiction originating in specific contexts and contextualising their analysis in the histories and cultures of those contexts. It is not surprising to see Latin American transfiction being the most frequently investigated case in this subgroup (36.4% of area-specific studies). The paramount importance of translation in Latin American cultures has been addressed by several scholars (Arrojo 2014; Cleary 2021; Gentzler 2008; Giraldo and Piracón 2023; Kripper 2023; Pagano 2002; Strümper-Krobb 2022; Valdeón 2011), with translation being held to be 'not a trope but a permanent condition in the Americas' (Gentzler 2008, 5). '[I]t was in Brazil', as Woodsworth and Lane-Mercier (2018, 1) point out, 'that attention was first drawn to a new 'turn' in translation studies', which was then labelled 'fictional turn'.

2.4.1 Why Cases?

When a case study of transfiction focuses on one text, it is referred to here as 'single-case study', whereas when two or more sources are taken into consideration, a case study is described as 'multiple', following the terminology proposed by Susam-Sarajeva (2009). The corpus includes fifty-five publications presenting multiple case studies of transfiction and thirty-five publications presenting single cases. The dominance of case-based research in transfiction reflects 'the way that much translation studies research takes place today' (Hadley 2023, 12). A characteristic of the corpus of transfiction publications under scrutiny that does not align with existing patterns in Translation Studies is the specific type of case studies. While Susam-Sarajeva (2009, 43) noted that multiple case studies are rarely conducted in the field, 48.7% of the corpus under analysis is made up of multiple case studies. These come with more advantages than single cases 'in terms of the rigour of the conclusions which can be derived from them' (Susam-Sarajeva 2009, 44).

Whereas the reasons behind an introduction or a handbook chapter may be more directly identifiable with contextualising the research area and introducing or justifying a special issue or a book-length publication, the choice of the case study design in the corpus is often left unjustified. Therefore, even remaining cognisant of the different understandings and consequent implementations of case studies, the question remains: why cases?

A more or less conscious appeal to tradition, whereby researchers in transfiction continue to produce case studies simply because this has historically been the most frequently adopted design in this specific subfield and in Translation Studies in general might help answer this question. However, it would be, at the same time, quite a facile solution, as well as a logical fallacy on the part of the researchers involved.

A more likely reason could be found in the scope of the phenomenon. Despite the 'veritable boom of translation and interpreting as literary themes and of translators and interpreters as characters that is no longer limited to certain literary or cinematographic genres' (Kaindl 2014, 4), the actions of translator-characters in creative texts can be more or less apparent and/or pivotal in the unfolding of a plot. In this respect, Wakabayashi points out that relevant passages in her sources were 'fairly isolated references' in comparison to the initial corpus of texts she had identified (2011, 88). Ben-Ari (2010, 225) makes a similar observation, noting how passages dedicated to translation in her corpus of transfictional sources can be limited to 'a few passing remarks'. If combined with the fact that transfiction is not marketed as a distinct genre, it could be the case that, at least in the early stages of this research area, finding instances of transfiction was enough to ignite researchers' curiosity. It is perhaps this often 'serendipitous stumbling' (Wakabayashi 2011, 101) into translation scenes that has resulted in most transfiction research developing as a long series of more or less scattered case studies. In other words, scenes of translations might be perceived as curious cases worth investigating in isolation or in small groups precisely for their perceived singularity. If these hypotheses are correct, transfiction researchers would follow the rationales behind single case studies outlined by Susam-Sarajeva (2009, 44), who justifies them when they are 'necessary to disprove a theory', or considered to be 'extreme' or 'unique', or somehow 'revelatory'. However, as pointed out earlier, the reasoning behind the choice of the case design is hardly ever explained in the corpus.

Another factor that may have influenced researchers to examine transfiction by means of case studies is the legacy of Comparative Literature in Translation Studies as a 'polydiscipline' cross-fertilised by a wide gamut of neighbouring, mostly text-based fields (Gambier 2018, 182). The tendency to focus on cases is directly linked to the use of methods that can facilitate the interpretation of a relatively small amount of text, such as those passages of a narrative where translators are portrayed. In Literary Studies 'the practices of close reading have operated ... not as one method among others but as virtually definitive of the field' (Herrnstein Smith 2016, 58). This state of affairs is arguably reflected in Translation Studies as far as small-scale contrastive analyses between source and target texts are concerned, as well as transfiction research, where primary sources may not revolve entirely around translators. Close reading of literary texts has resulted in researchers grappling with the peculiarities of individual texts containing scenes of translation and taking them as cases, rather than identifying the underlying characteristics of transfiction as a phenomenon per se. This observation leads the discussion on to the methodologies employed in transfiction research over the last thirty years.

2.5 Methodologies

In the final chapter of the area-defining volume *Transfiction*, Spitzl (2014, 366) justifies a flexible methodological approach in researching transfiction, 'an undisciplined encounter of approaches and methods, of *bricolage* (cf. Levi-Strauss 1966: 19), and multimodal eclecticism'. The same flexibility was echoed more recently by Delabastita (2020, 194), who recommends researchers resist 'any undue striving for mono-disciplinary isolation', because '[n]either the recourse to fictional texts nor the acute awareness of multilingualism and interculturality is an exclusive property of translation studies. Hence the need for a permanent dialogue with neighbouring fields such as literary studies, film studies, contact linguistics and multilingualism studies'.

Although this methodological eclecticism has been theoretically justified, during the categorisation process of this research the fact emerged that methodological approaches and specific methods are hardly ever spelled out. So, readers are not given a reason as to what the affordances of this eclecticism

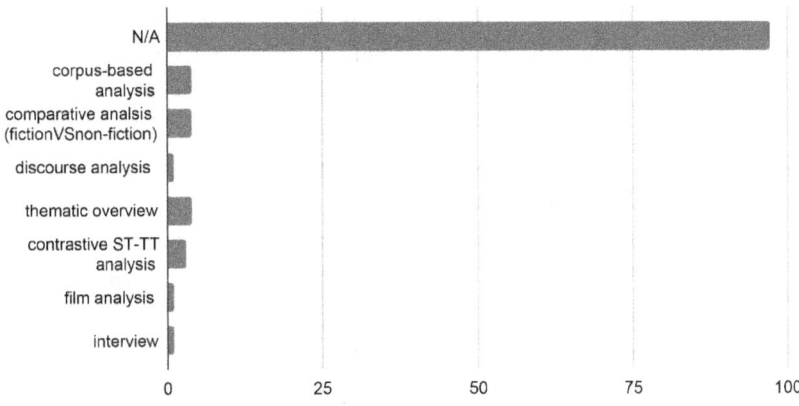

Figure 7 Methodologies

may be and, consequently, how or in what other cases it may prove useful. This issue has been observed in other Translation Studies meta-research, too. In their meta-analysis of collaborative learning in translation and interpreting, Du and Salaets (2025, 7) note that 'about half of the studies did not specify which specific analysis method was followed'. This percentage is dramatically higher in the corpus of transfiction research analysed here, where 97 research outputs (84.3%) do not specify what their methodological approaches and/or procedures are. These are labelled 'N/A', as illustrated in Figure 7, because no straightforward methodology or set of methods were identifiable either in the abstract or in the introduction section of the respective publication.

Before finding possible explanations for the distinct lack of clearly defined methodologies, the other categories represented in Figure 7 are introduced:

- 'Corpus-based analyses' (3.5%) are labelled this way because their respective authors explicitly mention the term 'corpus', as they all draw on a body of literature appearing to count at least thirty transfictional sources. Whether computational methods were used in analysing these sources, as the use of the term 'corpus' may suggest, is left to interpretation, as the authors do not disclose or reflect on the specific methods they employed. Likewise, they do not systematically provide forms of quantification. So, 'corpus-based' is likely to refer to a relatively large number of primary sources, as opposed to methods derived from corpus linguistics.
- While comparison in general can be taken as an inherent component of multiple case studies, 'comparative analysis (fiction VS non-fiction)' (3.5%) refers to publications that compare the fictional treatment of translation and translators with their non-fictional representations.

- 'Thematic overviews' (3.5%) as a methodological approach differ from the 'thematic overview' as a research design. As a design, thematic overviews discuss a series of themes found in conjunction with transfiction without engaging closely with individual primary sources. As a methodology, 'thematic overviews' are provided in the context of case studies, which are typically multiple case studies where each source is examined in detail. Therefore, these publications present the researchers' argumentation propped up by examples. This approach is flagged as problematic by Susam-Sarajeva (2009, 41), who explains that 'when a unit of analysis is treated as an example, it serves the general claims of the scholarly publication, as the author 'filters out' those examples which best support his/her main arguments'.
- 'Contrastive ST-TT analyses' (2.6%) include research comparing transfiction sources and their translations.
- 'Discourse analysis', 'film analysis', and 'interview' each represent 0.9% of the corpus, with each approach being found in 1 publication. In particular, 'film analysis' does not refer only to films being primary sources, but to the use of methods derived from Film Studies.

2.5.1 Wading the N/A

The fact that the vast majority of publications in the corpus do not directly describe any specific methodological procedures raises a series of questions. Is a missing methodology indicative of researchers not considering it as an essential part of an abstract and/or an introduction section? Or does transfiction research follow a certain methodology that has become so entrenched over time that it does not need an explicit description? Are primary sources taken as more relevant than the methods used to examine them? What could N/A look like, in practice?

A methodological approach that is not captured explicitly, but can be inferred from the overview of research designs is 'comparison'. 48.7% of the corpus is made up of multiple case studies that engage with two or more primary sources. In bringing multiple sources together, a phenomenon is observed from the different perspectives offered by each source, so that a comparison of some kind between these materials is unavoidable, whether this is directly addressed or not.

Kaindl (2018a, 52) observes that '[m]uch like translation is seen as a multi-disciplinary concept ..., the question of its fictional representation is also the subject of various disciplinary approaches – each with their own research questions and methodologies'. Considering the influence of Literary Studies on transfiction research, it might follow that close reading has also had a strong impact on the way transfiction has been examined. If close reading has been 'virtually definitive of the field' (Herrnstein Smith 2016, 58), then researchers straddling Comparative Literature and Translation Studies might have resorted to close reading techniques by default when analysing translator stories. Cronin (2009, 94) reports that '[i]t is generally accepted in translation pedagogy that all good translation involves close reading'. In this scenario, close reading appears to be a tacit methodological agreement in transfiction research. This seems to be the case even when transfiction research operates on a relatively large body of materials, rather than employing distant reading or other methods, as hypothesised for the 'corpus-based analysis' category. This seemingly automatic approach is not exclusive to the research areas considered here. '[H]owever, this particular methodology is often exempt from discussion when we reflect upon our methods', even though it is 'closely connected to the development of hermeneutics' and how we glean meaning out of texts (Ohrvik 2024, 240, 242). Existing definitions of close reading revolve around 'the practice of... examining closely the language of a literary work or a section of it' (Culler 2010, 20), with a focus on paratexts, stylistic idiosyncrasies, intertextuality, multiple meanings, and other rhetorical devices (Culler 2010, 22; Klarer 2004, 86; Ohrvik 2024, 250; Rigney 2019, 109). This diverse set of indications suggests that the umbrella term 'close reading' conflates a series of understandings and procedures hinging on the scrutiny of text. Some of these procedures are laid out by Kaindl (2014, 15–16), who pins down one aspect around which the organisation and analysis of materials can then revolve. These pivotal aspects include genre, historical and cultural contexts, single authors or groups of writers, and topics and functions associated with translation as a theme.

If close reading is taken as an umbrella term, then it could be hypothesised that related practices are referred to using a variety of hyponyms or synonyms. Likewise, it may be the case that other methodological approaches, such as 'comparison', are facilitated by close reading practices. The correlation of the verbs expressing the statement of purpose in each publication with the methodologies discussed earlier offers further room for interpretation. The fifteen verbs that recur more frequently in connection with the aim of each publication in the corpus are shown in Figure 8.

These verbs can be classified into three subgroups, based on how clearly they reflect the research methodology of their publication:

1) Most publications tend to express vague statements of purpose, seeking to 'examine' (21.8%), 'explore' (14.5%), 'investigate' (9.1%), 'analyse' (8.2%), 'discuss' (7.3%), 'reflect on' (1.8%), or 'look at' (0.9%) a phenomenon

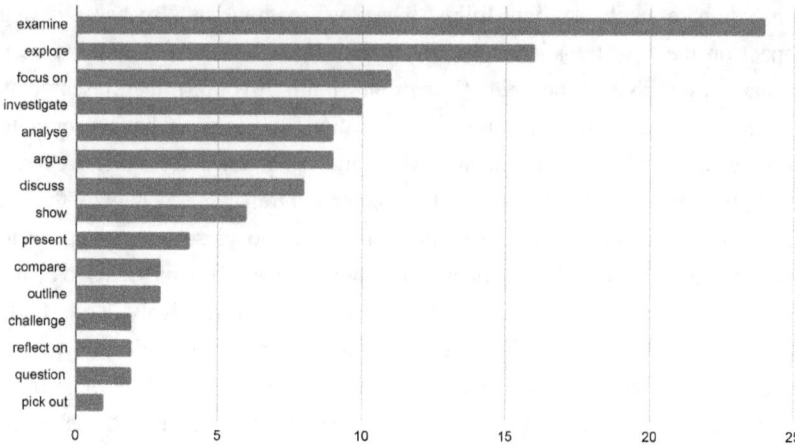

Figure 8 Statements of purpose

related to transfiction, as opposed to providing the reader with a clear sense of direction. This subgroup of publications arguably aims to tease out and interpret textual idiosyncrasies, as opposed to adopting one or a series of clear-cut methods.

2) A much smaller subgroup gathers verbs that convey a more concrete methodological orientation, such as 'compare' (2.7%), 'challenge' (1.8%) and 'question' (1.8%), 'test' (0.9%) and 'contrast' (0.9%). This second subgroup appears to reflect best practices in the adoption of case studies, namely their implementation for the purpose of challenging existing theories and findings (Hadley 2023, 10; Saldanha and O'Brien 2013, 209; Susam-Sarajeva 2009, 41, 44) based on characteristics that disprove these theories.

3) Another subgroup is made up of verbs that may be taken as indicative of the researcher seeking to convince their readers, rather than involving them in a process of gradual discovery. These include the verbs 'argue' (8.2%), 'show' (5.5%), 'present' (3.6%), 'outline' (2.7%), and 'suggest' (0.9%). In this respect, it is also noteworthy that only 10 publications ask an explicitly formulated research question, which is traditionally conceived as 'central in all research' (Meister 2018, 69), as well as a rhetorical means of involving the reader (Dontcheva-Navratilova 2021, 22; Hyland 2001, 569). These findings may suggest that this cross section of transfiction research has tended to rely on argumentation as an overarching methodology and has aimed to be persuasive, rather than being presented in an exploratory or heuristic style.

The identification of methods and methodologies raises questions about the materials that transfiction researchers have acted on. What have these methods been applied to? And what are the sources and the authors that transfiction research has engaged with over the last thirty years?

2.6 Primary Sources and Their Authors

As discussed earlier, the scope of what constitutes fiction in this research area is broad, ranging from written narratives to audiovisual materials, and spanning a variety of genres, from detective stories to science fiction. Whereas rigid distinctions between genres are problematised by several factors, such as genre-bending works, translingualism, and the nuances that characterise forms of life writing, more definite distinctions can be made based on the medium through which literature comes to fruition and is presented to readers. The English-language materials captured by this meta-analysis, hence, were categorised as follows: 'novels' (55.9%), 'short stories' (22%), 'films' (7.9%), 'poetry' (3.1%), 'TV series' and 'historical accounts' (2.4% each), and 'non-fiction', 'autobiographical texts', and 'novels + adaptations' (1.6% each). Less represented categories include 'musicals' and 'religious texts' (0.8% each), as shown in Figure 9.

The fact that novels are the most frequently used type of primary source in transfiction research mirrors a trend in world literature research, which has privileged the novel and other 'fictional genres', including short stories, at the expenses of other genres, such as autobiographical texts and other subgenres of non-fiction (Lenart-Cheng and Luca 2025, 5).

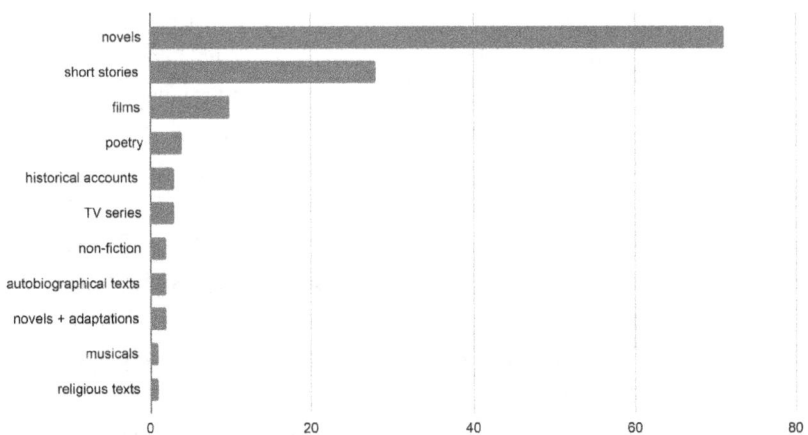

Figure 9 Primary sources

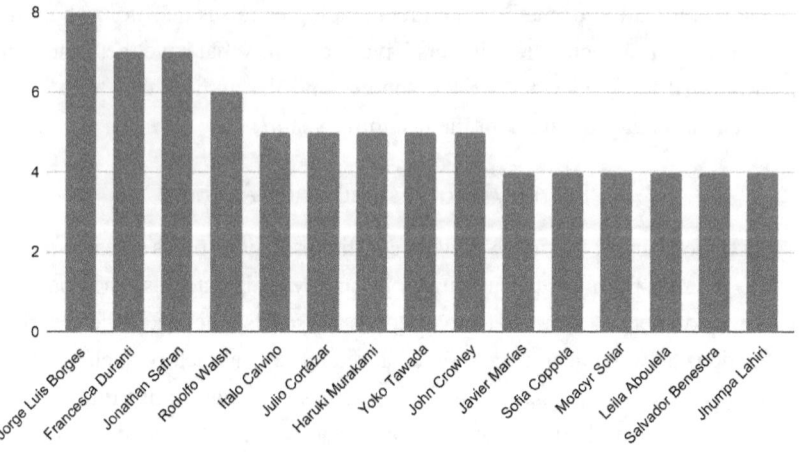

Figure 10 Authors of most frequent primary sources

Directly related to the categorisation of the materials used in transfiction research is the identification of the authors whose work has been the object of analysis in this field of enquiry. The fifteen authors whose work transfiction researchers have chosen to analyse most frequently are ranked in Figure 10.

There is little wonder why Borges is the most represented author in the corpus, given that his work 'is everywhere concerned with the theme of translation' (Gentzler 2008, 110) and, therefore, taken as quintessential for 'the reading of fiction as a space of theorization', especially in light of poststructuralist translation theories (Arrojo 2018, 4–6). Borges, however, belongs to a subgroup of three other Argentinian writers whose work happens to be a recurrent source in transfiction research, namely Rodolfo Walsh, Julio Cortázar, and Salvador Benesdra. It is significant that this quartet feeds into a whole cohort of writers from Latin America, whose histories, stories, culture, and scholars have deeply influenced transfiction and its academic scrutiny.

Other patterns among these fifteen authors are their thematisation of postmodern concerns, exemplified among others by Italo Calvino, and literary translingualism (or exophony), a practice shared by Yoko Tawada and Jhumpa Lahiri. In addition, many of them are both writers and translators, such as Haruki Murakami, Yoko Tawada, Javier Marías, Italo Calvino, and Jhumpa Lahiri. This finding aligns with a pattern already observed in transfiction studies of authors of transfiction often having lived experience as (literary) translators (Ben-Ari 2010, 235; Kaindl 2014, 8; Kripper 2023, 111; Strümper-Krobb 2009, 7, 177).

What stands out the most, however, is that almost all these authors are known for writing short stories and novels belonging to a variety of subgenres, ranging from autobiographical texts to experimental prose. This is indicative of the almost complete reliance of transfiction researchers on prose and written accounts, with the exception of Sofia Coppola's film *Lost in Translation* (2003).

2.7 Discussion

The first question guiding the research presented in this Element is about existing patterns in transfiction research. To answer this question, the Element has gone beyond the case study design, which has characterised the field to date, to present a meta-analysis of this research area, with a view to mapping its development from 1995 to 2025 in terms of how it has evolved, the themes it has addressed, and the research designs, methods, and materials of which it has made use.

Transfiction research appears to have developed discontinuously, mostly in combination with special issues and edited collections originating from academic conferences. Peaks in number of publications, rather than steady growth or extended plateaus, suggest that research in the field is spurred by the concerted effort of a relatively small group of researchers, as opposed to transfiction being a homogeneously and/or widely researched topic in Translation Studies.

In time, this research area has addressed a variety of topics, which range from translator invisibility and agency to localisation and language mediation in the Potterverse. Topics with greater frequency, however, tend to be of a theoretical or philosophical nature, like 'identity', 'fidelity' and 'infidelity', 'visibility' and 'invisibility', 'authorship', and 'ideology', which reflect thematic constellations and debates that are by now well-known in Translation Studies. Therefore, while transfiction does not appear to occupy a central position in the Translation Studies publishing landscape, the themes transfiction research has grappled with echo those themes that have historically informed a philosophically inclined cross section of Translation Studies. This is especially the case in the wake of poststructuralism and other phenomena of a transnational scope, such as migration and globalisation, as well as questions of belonging and metaphorical or practical self-translation.

This propensity for theoretical subjects that resist quantification may be argued to have influenced the methodological approaches adopted in transfiction research, which to date has depended on qualitative methods that are hardly ever described within a cohesive and clearly outlined methodology. These observations on the methodological aspects of transfiction research may point to a research process that does not take its cue from a research question, aiming to identify the best methodological workflow and materials to answer it (cf. Borg 2023, 47, 67; Meister 2018, 69), but hinges on the texts being analysed. So, instead of pinning down a research question based on which methods and materials of analysis are then selected, transfiction research appears to have focused thoroughly on translator stories per se, rather than using these stories to fill preidentified gaps in knowledge. This preference is reflected in the space dedicated to describing primary sources in existing publications, which tends to be larger than that dedicated to methodological aspects. This tendency is arguably reflected in Spitzer's conceptualisation of transfiction as a '*bordering approach* to theorizing translation, inextricably in relation with diverse areas and approaches' (2023, 3; emphasis in the original). There are advantages and disadvantages associated with this approach. The resulting conflation of methods and primary sources facilitated by close reading practices has been a powerful means of engaging thoroughly with individual narratives and the diverse topics and perspectives these narratives thematise. Addressing the peculiarities of each text, this approach has led to challenging translation clichés, tropes, and fallacious concepts, such as the notions of 'original' (e.g., Arrojo 2018), 'L1' (e.g., Sepp 2018), and 'mistranslation' (Kripper 2023), problematising simplistic and/or prescriptive assumptions on translation.

However, this research style based on regular engagement with individual texts has precluded systematic observations of how transfiction materials are analysed and what can be done differently with them within and outside transfiction research. The same tendency has resulted in 79.7% of transfiction research taking the form of case studies. This situation is likely to be observed also in other areas of Translation Studies, where manifestations of a certain phenomenon have led to the formulation of hypotheses, rather than more robust theories based on the findings of each case. Retranslation arguably exemplifies this tendency. In the case of transfiction, cumulative findings of case studies have been harnessed to connect the fictional representation of translators to other knowledge domains, including historiography, anthropology, and pedagogy, corroborating the idea that fiction can be used as a complementary source and/or a starting point for generating new theories and recontextualising existing ones. While case studies offer the possibility of exploring select primary sources in detail and identifying the features associated with fictional translators, if employed by default, they may prevent yielding impactful findings, and/or novelty in the field more generally.

After thirty years of transfiction research in which case studies have held sway, novelty, rather than repetition, is needed to revitalise this area of enquiry, as well as making transfiction useful for other areas of Translation Studies. Having identified these patterns in the ways knowledge is produced in transfiction research, the Element moves on to answer its next research questions: How can transfiction research diversify the design and methodologies that have traditionally informed this area of enquiry? And what benefits could this diversification bring?

3 New Research Avenues

The meta-analytical design adopted for this research has captured the state of the art of transfiction research to date, identifying how knowledge has been produced and shared in this subfield of Translation Studies. As a comprehensive design, meta-analyses are also a powerful tool to identify patterns and lacunae in existing studies and, consequently, act as a springboard for opening new research avenues and opportunities that future research can then develop further. Based on the patterns and lacunae discussed in the previous section, new research directions are outlined here so that, by diversifying traditional methods and materials, future transfiction research can expand its scope and inform other areas of Translation Studies.

3.1 Participant-based Methods

Transfiction research has tended to connect translator narratives with wider philosophical concerns. Accordingly, translation has been interpreted as 'a master metaphor … evoking the human search for a sense of self' (Delabastita and Grutman 2005, 23), and fiction's potential to give visibility to 'the personal, emotional investments' connected to translating has been emphasised (Arrojo 2018, 133). Recurrent themes in transfiction revolve around human translators, rather than translation as an abstraction or the technicalities of interlinguistic transfer. This human-centred perspective on transfiction has been argued to counterbalance the 'dehumanization of theories and concepts' in Translation Studies (Spitzl 2014, 365), fitting into a humanising trend in translation research that brings the translator as a person centre stage (Chesterman 2021, 2009; Ivancic 2022; Kaindl 2021, 2025). However, these observations in transfiction research rely on fictional translators, as opposed to real-world translators, which problematises this argument. Like translation, transfiction does not happen in a vacuum: it is the product of creative writers who in many cases have first-hand translation experience. Involving these writers through participant-based methods would enormously benefit research in the field, offering insights into how transfiction is generated, what its authors' motivations are for thematising translation and portraying translator-characters, and what their perceptions and understandings of translation are. Involving authors who portray fictional translators in multiple narratives may lead to identifying analogies in their own background, as well as the similarities their stories share. Interviews with authors of transfiction, therefore, would lead to humanising a research field that has brought human translators as characters centre stage, but has had little to no direct engagement with those writers who create transfiction in the first place. As shown in Figure 7, interviews account only for 0.9% of the methodologies found in the corpus, as a complementary method in one publication out of 113. Questions may include: What inspires you to write fiction about translators? Have you ever worked as a translator? Would you describe your work as autobiographical? Ultimately, participatory research in transfiction studies may also contribute to bridging the notorious gap between translation practice and translation theory (see Grass 2023, 9, 19, 67).

Similarly, transfiction research has not engaged with readers of transfiction, who could be asked about their motivations for reading translator stories, and whether these stories have in any way influenced their understanding of what translators do. Thus, interviewing and/or circulating questionnaires among these readers could provide a basis to tackle matters related to the phenomenon's impact on readers' lay or informed perception of translators and their work, which would consequently introduce quantitative methods into transfiction research.

Another pattern emerging from this meta-analysis is that transfiction research has appeared with high frequency after dedicated conferences, suggesting that some form of academic collaboration is what stimulates research in this area and propels its dissemination. However, this does not necessarily imply a synchronised research vision within the scholarly community of transfiction researchers. In addition, conferences are not the only collaborative context from which new knowledge can derive. Focus groups and roundtable discussions with transfiction researchers could become a fruitful occasion for concentrated participatory research, broadening knowledge in and of the field, as opposed to individual researchers continuing to dedicate their time to texts perceived as 'revelatory' or 'extreme' (Susam-Sarajeva 2009, 44). Interviews with transfiction researchers may also complement this and future meta-analyses. Interviews would contribute to humanising the field and contextualising findings, as well as completing the bigger picture of transfiction research with researchers' personal motivations and what they perceive as undiscovered areas of transfiction which they would suggest future research explore (see Güércio 2025, 28). Gathering information from readers, authors, and researchers of transfiction would ultimately offer a solid basis to go beyond a comparison of two authors and texts and, instead, substantiate a triangulation of viewpoints.

3.2 Novels Are Not the Only Sources

Another way of fostering a humanised approach to transfiction research without necessarily involving participants directly is by collating and analysing readers' reviews of transfiction sources, especially on websites and blogs dedicated to literature. This approach can be implemented by using methods derived from the Digital Humanities, such as web scraping (McDonough Dolmaya 2024, 66–73). These methods would facilitate forms of quantification as a complementary practice to the interpretivist approach that has traditionally informed studies in transfiction, leading to more solid results. In addition, the introduction of quantitative methods could open a conversation between transfiction and reception studies, making a pathway to factor in matters of impact in this research area.

Readers' reviews are not the only materials left out of transfiction research, which has been unduly restricted to prose, notably novels, while leaving other genres widely under-explored. Poetry, theatre pieces, and audiovisuals in general have received less attention, as shown in Figure 9, as did newer forms of literary expressions that may include translation as a theme, such as blogs, electronic literature, and other digital spaces. One of the questions that remain unanswered to date is whether specific genres affect the characterisation of translator characters. Exploring different primary sources may lead to correlating the features of these characters with the genres in which they are found. More specifically, future research could organise and explore transfiction materials adopting a genre-specific approach, and focusing on specific subgenres (Kaindl 2014, 15). For example, while thematic overviews of transfiction have been provided in conjunction with detective stories and science fiction (Mossop 1996, 2023; Strümper-Krobb 2013; Wozniak 2014), very little has been said about transfiction in other genres, such as children's literature or climate fiction.

Other underrepresented sources are constituted by translations of transfiction, with forms of contrastive analysis accounting for 2.6% of the methodologies found in the corpus. Keeping in mind that translation is highly context-bound (Hermans 2022, vii–viii) and that literary criticism is prone to equating translations to their sources (Arrojo 2010, 53; Hadley and Akashi 2015, 471), looking at translated transfiction would open a window into the ways translatorial practices are represented and adapted from one literary tradition to the other. This research direction can be broken down into several sub-units, taking into account not only direct translations, but also other paths, such as retranslations, indirect translations, and pseudotranslations, as well as adaptations.

3.3 From Individual Texts to Corpora and Lists

While offering the opportunity to analyse individual literary texts in depth, close reading may not allow researchers to grasp patterns across larger groups of primary sources that go beyond the usual scope of multiple case studies. So, how can evidence-based conclusions on transfiction as a phenomenon be drawn beyond specific texts, genres, and contexts? Instead of dividing materials into small groups to be analysed by means of close reading, primary sources in transfiction research may be analysed collectively through distant reading, making sure to observe all copyright constraints placed on the use of these materials. Techniques and methods based on distant reading would make it possible to investigate a high number of transfiction sources, transcending and/or combining designs with a traditionally restricted scope (cf. Holmes 1972/2000, 178–181). The use of computational methods would allow us to identify patterns both through a synchronic and a diachronic approach, including language distribution, genres, publication years, trends in titling, and possible relations between book covers, titles, and the stories they introduce. For instance, computational methods might facilitate sentiment analysis, extracting the emotional connotations conveyed by text automatically, instead of manually (Rebora 2023). Sentiment analysis across a large corpus of transfictional texts could support or challenge the negativity that typically accompanies fictional translators elicited by existing research (e.g., Ben-Ari 2010, 221; Ben-Ari 2014, 122; Delabastita and Grutman 2005, 23; Godbout 2014, 186). A combination of close reading and distant reading could possibly strike a balance between specificity and little generalisability on the one hand, and the detection of overarching and/or otherwise hardly perceptible patterns at the expense of context on the other (see Youdale 2020, 6–7).

Working with corpora of transfiction, as well as lists of transfictional works, instead of a relatively small selection of texts, can reveal patterns across instances of transfiction that are not identifiable through close engagement with one or a modest number of narratives. Software generating frequency lists and concordances can also help researchers visualise these findings (McDonough Dolmaya 2024, 109). In addition, working with lists may curb the risk of confirmation bias, which might influence the choice of primary sources chosen to develop case studies. Working with lists may also lead to generating hypotheses that can then be tested through closer engagement with a group of representative cases, but may not be formulated based on single case studies.

3.4 Pedagogical Scenarios and Collaborative Practices

Lists of transfiction works can be found in the 'references' section and appendixes of existing publications (e.g., Kaindl 2014, 20–21; Querido 2011, 207–209), as well as online. The most complete and up-to-date list of works of transfiction is arguably 'Traductores en la literatura: lista de obras' [Translators in literature: a list of works], published in *Vasos comunicantes*, an online journal curated by ACE Traductores.[5] These lists can be used as pedagogical resources, not only from a theoretical perspective, but also to stimulate students to actively and practically engage with materials of different kinds and formats beyond typical written narratives. Lists lend themselves to be used in the context of workshops, hackathons, and other project-based classes with undergraduate and postgraduate students who are not necessarily familiar with transfiction, but have an interest in literature and translation. This practical, collaborative scenario would complement other text-based pedagogical uses of transfiction, whereby translator stories are taken as a spurring point to discuss translation-related phenomena (Arrojo 2010; Cleary 2021; Kripper 2023). At the same time, working with these resources, as opposed to individual texts, would lead students to develop transferable skills, sharpening their teamwork, research, and pattern recognition competencies.

Exploring these lists and cataloguing their patterns may also generate new hypotheses. For instance, it may reveal that the authors whose works are the most frequently analysed in transfiction research may not be the same authors whose names recur more frequently in these lists. If this is the case, new research avenues can be opened by taking into account the works found in these lists, as opposed to reusing well-known sources. More importantly, involving students in these collaborative activities could work as a way of incorporating transfiction into the Translation Studies curriculum, contributing to a higher visibility of transfiction among students and early-career researchers, who may then advance knowledge of the phenomenon in their future research. A work-in-progress repository of online lists of transfiction sources is presented in Table 3.

---

[5] Their website is accessible here: https://vasoscomunicantes.ace-traductores.org/ (last accessed 24 July 25).

Table 3 Online lists of transfiction works

Title	Curated by/published in	URL	Notes
Traductores en la literatura: lista de obras	Vasos Comunicantes – Revista de ACE Traductores	https://vasoscomunicantes.ace-traductores.org/2024/04/10/los-traductores-en-la-literatura-lista-de-obras/	Initiated by Núria Viver, with notes on each item by Daniel Najmías.
Fiction about Translators (Trans-Fiction)	Goodreads	www.goodreads.com/list/show/85566.Fiction_About_Translators_Trans_Fiction_	60 items. List created in 2015.
Books Featuring Translators	Goodreads	www.goodreads.com/list/show/103006.Books_featuring_Translators	30 items. List created in August 2016.
Translators/Interpreters in Fiction	Goodreads	www.goodreads.com/list/show/84778.Translators_Interpreters_in_Fiction_	65 items. List created in 2015 and edited in 2018.
10 Translated Books about Translators for International Translation Day	Words Without Borders. The Home for International Literature	https://wordswithoutborders.org/read/article/2021-09/10-translated-books-about-translators-for-international-translation-day/	10 translated books about translators from Japan, Denmark, Mexico, Lebanon, and more. Published 30 September 2021.
List of Language Interpreters in Fiction	Wikipedia	https://en.wikipedia.org/wiki/List_of_language_interpreters_in_fiction	Last edited in March 2024. A list of fictional characters by occupation compiled by Wikipedia users is also available.
Books that include Translators as Characters	ProZ.com	https://wiki.proz.com/wiki/index.php/Books_that_have_translators_as_characters	This article was inspired by the forum post 'Translators as characters in fiction books', posted by Rafaela Lemos in 2008.

Reading List: Translators in Literature	Blog 'in lieu of a field guide'	https://booktrek.blogspot.com/2011/12/reading-list-translation-in-fiction.html	Last updated in February 2024.
Novels with Language Professionals as Characters	Catharine Cellier-Smart – A Smart Translator's Reunion Blog Smart Translate	https://asmarttranslatorsreunion.wordpress.com/2012/07/11/a-few-books-with-linguists-as-characters/	Last updated in October 2021.
7 Novels Featuring Literary Translators as Characters	Arielle Burgdorf – Electric Lit	https://electricliterature.com/7-novels-books-portrayals-of-literary-translators-in-fiction/	Published 15 May 2024.
Interpreting and Interpreters in Movies	Sarah Bonanno Wolde – LinkedIn	www.linkedin.com/pulse/interpreting-interpreters-movies-sarah-bonanno-wolde/	Published 3 June 2017.
Films with a Linguist as the Lead Character	Quora	www.quora.com/Besides-%E2%80%9CArrival%E2%80%9D-are-there-any-other-films-with-a-linguist-as-the-lead-character	Last updated in 2019.

3.5 Transfiction between Literary Translator Studies and Genetic Translation Studies

While it is known that transfiction authors are very often translators, the systematic identification of differences between autobiographical transfiction and non-autobiographical transfiction – as well as of the criteria and parameters beyond explicit statements to ascertain whether and when transfiction can be described as autobiographical – are still open to interpretation. Related questions are whether there are factors beyond an author/translator's life path that may lead to the writing of transfiction, when transfiction happens in a writer's career, and what patterns can be drawn in this respect from existing cases. Research aiming to answer these questions could make use of and adapt methods and paradigms at the intersection of Literary Translator Studies and Genetic Translation Studies, with the former focusing on literary translators as individuals (Kaindl 2021), and the latter on 'the evolving phases of the writing process, of which the published text may be considered just a phase' (Nunes, Moura, and Pinto 2021, 2). Accordingly, transfiction authored by translators may be correlated with these writers' endogenetic and exogenetic materials, spanning personal notes and interviews. Taking into account potential correlations between writers' lives and careers and the creation of transfiction, this approach may also mitigate the risk of taking transfiction as a by-product or a reflection of a translator's own career (Strümper-Krobb 2021, 67–68; 2009, 177). The study of translators' endogenetic and exogenetic materials may benefit from the methodological steps outlined by Kaindl (2025, 335–336) in relation to auto/biographical, translator-centred research, ranging from the contextualisation of auto/biographical documents to their classification.

The methodological directions outlined in this section are not conceived as mutually exclusive. These approaches can be used together as part of a mixed methodological framework. For instance, participatory research can be complemented by forms of textual analysis, and corpora of transfiction can lay the basis for subsequent large-scale comparative studies. Similarly, the results of collaborative workshops and hackathons may become a springboard for establishing a network of transfiction researchers and achieving research objectives through teamwork.

4 What Translators Have to Say

This Element has proceeded along a logic of gradual abstraction, moving from attention to individual examples of transfiction to drawing the bigger picture of the research practices adopted in this subfield, irrespective of specific stories, authors, researchers, and literary and cultural contexts. In alignment with this logic, and expanding on the previous section, this last section lays out methodological possibilities for future research that may then be applied to a variety of research topics. It does so with a view to answering the third research question of this Element: How can transfiction materials be made useful for neighbouring research subfields of Translation Studies?

To an extent, this section takes the form of a thought experiment, as it works with hypotheses to imagine possible methods and identify sources, rather than acting directly on these sources. The aim is to retrieve information on what translators have to say about what they do and who they are, spanning fiction and non-fiction, and intersecting transfiction with (literary) Translator Studies. Accordingly, different accounts of translators' experiences can be used to 'confirm, correct or relativize our current understanding of translation and translators. In this respect, the theorization of the translatorial subject complements translation research' (Kaindl 2021, 22).

4.1 Old Questions and New Possibilities

In the fourth volume of *Linguistica Antverpiensia* dedicated to fictional representations of translators and multilingualism, Jean Anderson investigated the affective dimension to translation thematised in English- and French-language narratives. Anderson (2005, 181) came to the conclusion that

> until such time as we have access to more autobiographical and biographical accounts of literary translators which do explore affective aspects in depth, or to qualitative research in this area, we can only construct our hypotheses from fictional representations – recognising as we do so that they are only fiction, but looking closely at those elements which recur across several works and which in addition can be linked to existing research in related areas.

Unpacking this conclusion, other observations can be made on how Anderson envisioned future research on translators' subjectivity: (1) Transfiction can be used for want of a better option in terms of amenable sources, instead of taking it as a source worth investigating for its own specificity. (2) (Auto)biographical accounts would make for more suitable materials to explore translators' subjectivity. (3) Based on recurrent patterns in transfiction, hypotheses can be put forward, but these need to be supported by more qualitative research. Twenty years have passed since these limitations were outlined. What can be done now in transfiction research to explore what translators have to say about their lives and the behind-the-scenes literary translation work, as well as education and training, feelings, motivations and professional satisfaction that could not be done in 2005?

Instead of dismissing (trans)fiction as a lesser option and opting for an 'either/or' approach to the selection of primary sources and types of research, this last section outlines and tests a mixed methodological approach, collocating transfiction at the intersection of process-oriented and participatory translation research. The working hypothesis is that transfiction can be used to complement other sources in the study of literary translation as a profession and a process. Combining transfiction, translators' non-fiction, and the results of participant-based studies, this thought experiment ultimately seeks to identify innovative ways of substantiating triangulation, making transfiction useful for neighbouring research areas, such as Translator Studies.

4.2 Fiction, Non-fiction, and Literary Translation Processes

Information on translators' lives and work, ranging from their self-perceptions to the texts they translate and what happens in the process of translating them, has traditionally been garnered from participant-based methods, such as interviews, questionnaires, protocols, and ethnographic methods (see, e.g., Borg 2023, 5–9; Marin-Lacarta and Yu 2023, 151; Munday, Pinto, and Blakesley 2022, 90–91; Saldanha and O'Brien 2013, chapters 4 and 5). The reliance on human participants that characterises these studies can be at the same time a strength and a limitation. On the one hand, research hinging on human participation can counterbalance the historical tendency in translation research to focus on texts and linguistic abstractions by promoting a humanising approach (Kaindl 2021; Pym 2009). On the other hand, involving human translators, like any other form of human participation in research, comes with a series of challenges, ranging from ethical concerns to the difficulty of finding participants and the risk of low response rate (Saldanha and O'Brien 2013, 115, 153, 179). What could the role of translator stories be in this scenario?

The idea behind this experiment is that, as an example of written narratives revolving around translator-characters, transfiction can be considered as a valid source to complement research on translators' lives and aspects of their work, which substantiates the subfield of Translator Studies. Chesterman (2009, 16–17) sees in literary texts depicting translators a possible resource to explore sociological aspects, such as 'the public image of the translator's profession'. Transfiction is also connected to the cultural branch of Translator Studies, where it can work as a medium to analyse how translators are perceived in different cultures, including the stereotypes and attitudes associated with them

(Chesterman 2021, 242). Especially when evidence is available for the autobiographical nature of transfiction, these stories may be taken as an indirect source of information on translators and their work. In other words, transfiction may be counted among those extra-textual materials that offer '[c]rucial testimony about both the process of translation and the conditions under which it takes place', similar to 'post-hoc accounts by the individuals concerned, in the form of memoirs or autobiographies or interviews in which they consciously reflect on the event' (Munday 2014, 68).

The use of translators' 'personal accounts' for Translator Studies is also endorsed by Kaindl (2021, 10), who in *Transfiction* had already contemplated that '[g]oing beyond the fictional, we might also include (auto)biographies and memoirs of translators and interpreters or documentaries about translation and interpreting' (2014, 4). Other researchers have aligned themselves with this research direction, including Todorova (2014), Maier (2014), Ivančić and Zepter (2021), Eberharter (2021), and Borg (2023). In particular, Eberharter (2021, 74) highlights 'the fundamental ambiguity of biography as a genre and key issues related to biographical writing, such as the immanent fictionality of biography and the representation of facts in the biographical narrative'. Along similar lines, Eakin (2020, 7) argues that 'the allegiance to truth that is the central, defining characteristic of memoir' is to be understood as 'an allegiance to remembered consciousness and its unending succession of identity states, an allegiance to the history of one's self', rather than 'an allegiance to a factual record that biographers and historians could check'.

The absence of reliable means to ascertain or measure (non-)fictionality would automatically exclude transfiction from any applications beyond transfiction studies, if transfiction had to be taken as a source of distilled factual information (cf. Giraldo and Piracón 2023, 112, 123). Because 'it is a mistake to saddle literary texts with world-tracking representational function' (John 2016, 36), transfiction may be used in line with the '*epistemology of fiction*' elaborated by Schoeneborn and Cornelissen, who describe 'fictional realities (e.g., fictionalized art or narrative fantasies) as objects of inquiry in their own right' (2022, 140; emphasis in the original), as opposed to a 'plan B' option (cf. Anderson 2005, 181). This means, for instance, that transfiction may provide insights into the perceptions and self-perceptions of translators and their work, without the claim of scientific rigour. It may consequently complement more traditional materials and methods of enquiry in Translator Studies, (literary) translation processes, as well as having potential applicability beyond these contexts.

4.2.1 Translation Memoirs and Autobiographical Transfiction

'Literary translators are increasingly writing essays', points out Borg (2023, 32), 'in which they reflect on their own translation practices and processes'. A notable, recent example is Jen Calleja's *Fair: The Life-Art of Translation* (2025). These essays, typically written in the first person, are a literary phenomenon labelled as translator or translation memoir, and have been gathering momentum in Translation Studies as a form of creative-critical practice (Grass 2023; Grass and Robert-Foley 2024). Recent research in translation memoirs corroborates the conceptual basis for using transfiction outside transfiction studies. While the theoretical framework outlined earlier challenges clear-cut distinctions between fiction and non-fiction, research on translation memoirs and translation as a creative-critical practice weakens the separation between translation practice and translation as an object of critical reflection (Calleja 2024; Grass 2023; Grass and Robert-Foley 2024). In particular, Grass (2023, 9–10) sees the translation memoir as a form of autobiographical writing that functions as a catalyst for 'autotheory', whereby 'theorising remains open to the twists and turns of its practice, an experiment in thinking with translation'. The use of translators' first-hand accounts for research purposes comes with inherent limitations, such as limited generalisability, but also presents a series of affordances. Reflecting on these affordances, Borg (2023, 32) points out that '[a]lbeit mostly non-empirical, these writings provide interesting insights into literary translators' processes, approaches and practices' that are especially useful in Cognitive Translation Studies, in the context of which literary translation has not received much attention.

The same affordance may be presented by autobiographical transfiction, that is, transfiction authored by writers who also translate, especially when their translation experience informs their translator stories, with examples ranging from Jhumpa Lahiri (2015) to Luciano Bianciardi (1962/2019). This subcategory of transfiction may be compared to 'fictionalized content ... grounded in quasi-ethnographic work ..., and thus can provide researchers with in-depth insights into certain societal milieus that would otherwise be inaccessible or hard to capture and collect' (Schoeneborn and Cornelissen 2022, 152), in the same way translation memoirs can be read as forms of 'autoethnography' (Calleja 2024, 29). Both types of work emerge from lived experiences, so that theorising occurs through autobiography. Autobiographical transfiction, therefore, may be explored with a view to sounding out information on translators' background, job satisfaction, psychophysical responses, (self-)perception, and personality traits (see Kaindl

2021, 19), as well as eliciting information on the processes behind the writing of literary translations.

4.3 Mixing Materials and Methods: Transfiction for Triangulation

Schoeneborn and Cornelissen (2022, 140–141) outline three methodological approaches underpinning 'an epistemology of fiction':

1) Contrasting empirical studies with fictional and/or counterfactual statements to better understand reality;
2) Juxtaposing fictional and/or counterfactual statements with other interpretative scientific findings to test these statements;
3) Treating fictional and fictionalised narratives as empirical data, that is, as an object of enquiry per se.

In the context of this experiment, these approaches are not taken as mutually exclusive: all three could be employed concurrently, so that transfiction is not only taken as an object of analysis in itself, but can move outwards of transfiction studies to inform Translator Studies by triangulating information of a different nature.

Tackling methodological aspects of process-oriented translation research, Saldanha and O'Brien (2013, 109) highlight a 'consensus on the necessity of triangulation, the comparison of results from various methods, and a focus on process complemented by product analysis or vice versa'. Mellinger and Hanson (2021, 173) have reiterated this necessity, pointing out that qualitative approaches 'and triangulation that combines various forms of evidence' have complemented quantitative methods in the study of translation processes. The analysis of transfiction authored by translators may be taken as one source to substantiate triangulation in process-oriented literary translation research, intersecting with the results of participant-based studies and translators' life writing, as illustrated by Figure 11. This combination of methods and materials could lead not only to corroborating 'what was already found with one approach', but also to generating what Flick (2022, 663) calls 'extensions of knowledge', incorporating and dealing with possible divergences across the materials used.

Taking as an example a research scenario where two data sets are considered, Flick (ibid., 659) indicates as good practice 'to identify topics in both data sets, in which . . . differences become manifest and to compare both views by juxtaposing statements of both groups'. Little explanation is given in terms of how exactly these views are to be compared, but existing studies offer a reference point. Using translation diaries by Gregory Rabassa and Daniel Hahn as a source of external

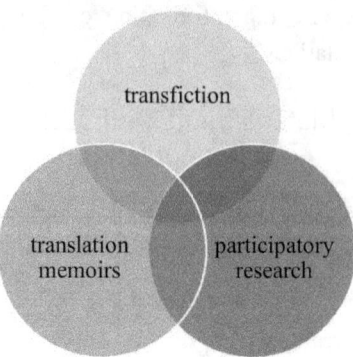

Figure 11 Triangulation of materials

evidence, Borg (2023, 141–142, 149, 152) identifies topics and behaviours described in these diaries, counts the drafting phases mentioned by their authors, and compares literary translation processes identified in her ethnographic study with how processes of the same nature are thematised in the diaries. The same approach may be extended to studies that adopt transfiction as a further primary source, along with translators' life writing and findings emerging from participatory research. To mirror this triangulation of materials, a triangulation of methods can be achieved by mixing the approaches outlined by Schoeneborn and Cornelissen (2022, 140–141), manual analysis and software-based analysis, as well as qualitative and quantitative methods.

4.4 Examples

The following two examples proceed by juxtaposing excerpts from autobiographical transfiction – with the author's practical or metaphorical experience of translation percolating through their fiction – alongside excerpts from translation memoirs and findings of participant-based research. Tables 4 and 5, therefore, present a somewhat gradual shift from fiction towards academic writing. Beyond predictable stylistic differences between creative and academic writing practices, each example aims to pinpoint one aspect of 'translatorial action' (Kaindl 2021, 6, 15) and its connotations across the three types of sources being considered. Precisely because these are examples, they should not be taken as a rigid methodological set-up for future research, but as a possible starting point to think about what this kind of triangulation might look like, in practice. The scale of these examples is limited to a maximum of three excerpts per type of source. Small-scale examples inevitably involve some cherry-picking, a risk which could be curbed by means of large-scale comparative analyses making use of the same three types of materials.

Table 4 Literary translation processes

Transfiction	Memoirs	Participatory research
a) 'There was a woman, a translator, who wanted to be another person .... Every time she remembered something of her past life, she was convinced that another version would have been better .... She wanted to produce another version of herself, in the same way that she could transform a text from one language into another' (Lahiri 2016, 67). b) '[I]l processo di tradurre me stessa, la mia identità, le mie tradizioni, in un contesto sconosciuto' [the process of translating myself, my identity, my traditions, into an unknown context] (Milkova 2022, 71).	a) 'I'm not immobile.... Neither I nor the writing I have published is immobile' (Briggs 2017/2021, 51). b) 'A translation does not develop smoothly, predictably, neatly .... The process shown in this book is not supposed to be instructional. It is merely a description of what I do .... Every translator's process will be different' (Hahn 2022, 17, 31). c) '[U]n aspetto soggettivo, ... personale ..., non generalizzabile' [a subjective, (...) personal aspect (...), not generalisable] (Bocchiola 2015, 11–12).	a) 'The findings, ... indicated that the number of phases in the translation process and their length might vary among translators and that this might be linked to their process profile. These challenge the subdivision of the translation process into three fixed phases' (Borg 2023, 175).

4.4.1 Example 1: Literary Translation Processes

This first example shows how the triangulation of primary sources outlined earlier may be applied to investigate literary translation processes, whether practically or metaphorically conceived. For instance, practical aspects of literary translation processes are represented by several rounds of drafting, while on the metaphorical level this process may be understood as a translation '*of* the self', as opposed to translation '*by* the self' (Gentes and

Table 5 Motivations and job satisfaction

Transfiction	Memoirs	Participatory research
a) '[È] un lavoro . . . parecchio faticoso e non piace . . .. Obiettivamente era un lavoro assai interessante perché ti consentiva di apprendere un mucchio di cose sugli argomenti più disparati'. [it's a rather tiring job (. . .) and disliked (. . .). Objectively, it was a very interesting job because it allowed you to learn a lot of things about the most diverse topics] (Bianciardi 1962/2019, 133, 138). b) 'Tanta gente considera il proprio lavoro come una punizione quotidiana. Io, invece, amo il mio lavoro di traduttore' [Many people consider their work a punishment. I, instead, love my work as a translator] (Lakhous 2006/2011, 155).	a) 'I love it. . . . I mention this because I'm not sure the diary you are about to read conveys how much I love it. There's, um, quite a lot of complaining. But don't be fooled' (Hahn 2022, 3). b) '[T]here *are* deep pleasures in translating' (Briggs 2017/2021, 91; emphasis in the original).	a) 'Previous studies on translators' and interpreters' job satisfaction highlight a paradox: translators and interpreters are often highly satisfied with the intrinsic nature of their work, but less satisfied with their professional status and working conditions (e.g., AIIC 2002; Dam and Zethsen 2016; Heino 2020; Ruokonen et al. 2020; Svahn 2020; see also Ruokonen and Svahn, this issue)' (Ruokonen, Svahn, and Heino 2024, 1–2). b) See also Dam and Ruokonen (2024, 84).

Van Bolderen 2022, 369; emphasis in the original). This suggests that literary translation processes can be subdivided into a variety of different categories, such as self-translation processes.

The excerpts collected in Table 4 show a gradual diversification of the terms in which literary translation processes are put. The two passages of autobiographical transfiction emphasise a metaphorical and existential dimension, with linguistic transfer and translators' workflows being eclipsed by introspection and personal observations. Excerpts from translation memoirs, instead, are more varied, with example 'a' being of a philosophical tone, and examples 'b' and 'c' revolving around the translator's subjectivity and its influence on the translation process. Both translation memoirs and transfiction appear to 'make visible ... the archive of hesitations, doubts, and errors, the personal and political negotiations that must happen in the record of translation subjects' travels between languages' (Grass and Robert-Foley 2024, 2). Academic literature emerging from participatory research echoes the other two sets of materials insofar as the element of unpredictability connected to the human factor is concerned. However, it naturally points to empirical observations on the practical aspects of the process, such as the number of drafts of the target text. This first example prompts questions about the possibility of developing a systematic framework to investigate phenomena related to literary translation processes.

Small-scale studies following this approach and hinging on one author/translator – set against the background of participatory research and compared with other authors/translators' transfiction and/or translation memoirs – would align with the humanised approach that informs Translator Studies, relying on the uniqueness of individual translators, instead of aiming primarily for homogeneity and generalisation (Kaindl 2021, 11–12). This kind of studies, hinging on a human component which is 'constantly shifting' (Robinson 1991, 21), could generate new ways of approaching the 'unfinalizable task' of studying translators as individuals (Kaindl 2021, 22). Large-scale comparative studies that go beyond single authors/translators, instead, may tease out recurrent patterns in each of the three types of sources, which may then be compared and visualised using dedicated software. This second approach may facilitate a shift from the study of individual translators and the processes they follow to a broader approach to the study of human translators' activity and cognition, which Risku (2024, 68) has called 'extended translator studies'.

4.4.2 Example 2: Motivations and Job Satisfaction

The textual materials underpinning the next example in Table 5 pivot on translators' satisfaction with their profession.

This second example is of a somewhat more straightforward interpretation than the first one. All excerpts point to the tension between the intellectual motivation and appreciation translators derive from their job and the challenges it poses, a clash between intrinsic motivation and work conditions or status. The two examples of transfiction, in particular, resonate with the different ways in which translation is perceived by literary translators and non-experts, whose understanding of translation 'usually clashes with the way literary translators see themselves' (Ruffo 2022, 20).

4.5 Strengths and Limitations

The tripartite approach described earlier presents strengths and limitations. On the one hand, triangulation based on (autobiographical) transfiction, translation memoirs, and findings of participatory research does not dismiss fiction as a lesser source. Instead, it harnesses its potential to provide social information (Carroll 2016, 84; Kaindl 2012, 146) and describe 'how people and their lives are found to be' (John 2016, 46). The combined analysis of autobiographical transfiction and translation memoirs can complement participant-based methods, notably questionnaires and surveys, which can remain depersonalised and/or anecdotal (cf. Dam and Zethsen 2016, 183; Maier 2014, 166; Sela-Sheffy 2005, 17). In addition, questionnaires can generate exploratory data, but may fail to provide explanatory information, unless complemented by other methods, such as interviews (Saldanha and O'Brien 2013, 152). In small-scale studies adopting this triangulation model, the results of participatory research can be enriched by insights into translators' emotional, cognitive, and professional dimension, as well as the processes through which translated literature comes to fruition. Large-scale studies of this kind, instead, can dilute anecdotal information within a corpus of textual materials which could result in conclusions not on specific authors/translators or texts, but on certain aspects of their profession.

At this initial stage, the most apparent limitation is the availability of materials describing the specific aspects of the translator profession or the translation process that researchers may want to investigate. While translation memoirs seem to be an increasingly popular genre, not every literary translator decides to write one, whether in the traditional form of a book-length publication or online. Transfictional works, instead, abound. But this does not necessarily imply that the aspect or topic that researchers aim to explore can be found in every text that qualifies as transfiction. In these cases, triangulation of materials is needed to gather enough material for analysis, as well as being a means of furthering rigour, especially in small-scale studies. Exploratory large-scale studies adopting this approach, instead, may make use of specific software to identify recurrent topics and subsequently proceed to analyse them. At the same time, online text analysis platforms may not recognise the topic selected for analysis because this may not occur with a high frequency in the corpus being explored. In this respect, Wakabayashi specified that relevant passages in her sources were 'fairly isolated references' in comparison with the initial corpus of texts she had compiled (2011, 88). Similarly, Ben-Ari (2010, 225) noted how passages dedicated to translation in her corpus of transfictional sources were often restricted to 'a few passing remarks'. This situation may be common to other texts that can be categorised as transfiction.

5 Conclusion

The spurring point for this Element was the sense of repetition and exhaustion expressed in exiting transfiction studies, either in relation to the nature of the primary sources being analysed or the way research in the field is generally conducted (see Ben-Ari 2014, 122; Bergantino 2024, 237; Strümper-Krobb 2022, 345). The Element has shown that this repetition can be traced back not to transfiction per se – which, beyond recurring tropes, is a result of human creativity – but to seemingly unquestioned practices of knowledge-building adopted in this area of enquiry over the last thirty years (1995–2025). Thus, the rationale for adopting a meta-analytical design is the need to take stock of the ways transfiction researchers have carried out their research and presented their findings, which consequently leads to the identification of patterns, as well as gaps in knowledge and future opportunities.

It has been found that transfiction research has relied heavily on case studies, a research design that, in time, has precluded the formulation of comprehensive theories and easily generalisable findings. The implication is not that the case study design is an inherently futile research practice, but that their unquestioned and continued implementation may become self-referential, instead of advancing the scope of research in transfiction. Thus, transfiction research in general would benefit from recontextualising, and possibly questioning, existing practices in the field, experimenting with other methods and materials. The second implication is that the long series of case studies would provide a solid basis for future research if their findings were systematically brought in conversation through meta-analyses with different designs and scope. In turn, future meta-research may reveal aspects of transfiction that are valid not just for a limited number of cases but are definitive of transfiction as a whole.

Despite being a much more comprehensive research design than the case study, which may be argued to represent the other end of a continuum, the meta-analysis presented by this Element is far from offering an ultimately complete picture of transfiction studies. Partly, this is the case due to some of the limitations observed in connection with meta-analytical designs, ranging from issues with the bibliographic search for data collection to information left out by the authors of published transfiction studies (cf. Bergantino and Hadley 2025, 34–35; Du and Salaets 2025, 14). The main reason, however, is that this specific meta-analysis was not set up with a view to synthesising what researchers have found out and/or hypothesised about transfiction as a phenomenon, but to catalogue the practices they have adopted to investigate the topic, come to certain conclusions, and disseminate their findings. This meta-analysis, hence, has resulted in a concentrated profile of transfiction studies, as opposed to a comprehensive and systematic synthesis of what we know about transfiction as an object of academic investigation. Future studies driven by this objective would enormously benefit transfiction studies, complementing the meta-analysis presented here by synthesising findings of existing case studies that populate research in the same field. Hoon refers to this kind of meta-synthesis as '*interpretation synthesis*' (2013, 526; emphasis in the original), acknowledging the researcher's interpretation informing case studies, and pointing to the necessity to synthesise the qualitative evidence they provide. While information on what is known about transfiction can be inferred by the research practices categorised in this Element, what exactly scholars have observed about fictional translators falls beyond the scope of this meta-analysis. At the same time, the meta-research presented here aims to work as a springboard for future research to engage with interpretation synthesis in Translation Studies within and outside transfiction. Hoon (2013, 527) describes interpretation synthesis as

> an exploratory, inductive research design to synthesize primary qualitative case studies for the purpose of making contributions beyond those achieved in the original studies. This is a meta-study because it involves the accumulation of previous case studies' evidence, and more specifically its extraction, analysis, and synthesis. Consequently, a meta-synthesis does not refer to the reuse of firsthand data stemming from the case researchers' own observations .... Instead, a meta-synthesis occurs at the level at which the original researchers of the primary studies have constructed their insights in accordance with their own understanding and interpretation of the data.

Put more simply, interpretation synthesis takes the form of qualitative meta-analyses, which allow researchers to take stock of and interpret findings across existing qualitative studies (Timulak and Creaner 2022, 555). To an extent, the principle behind this research design is necessary for any solid literature review. However, reviews in transfiction research have been narrative, rather than systematic. So, while they provide an exhaustive overview to contextualise the work they introduce, they may miss certain aspects of previous research in the same area that are not immediately relevant to the publication they contextualise. In addition, narrative reviews do not typically provide quantification for the topics and concerns they frame. Most topics that transfiction researchers have dealt with resist straightforward quantification, but this does not prevent future research from finding alternative ways of quantifying consensus on the existing interpretations of these topics, identifying different, possibly recurrent, perspectives from which they have been explored, and categorising the contribution to knowledge of individual case studies. Qualitative meta-analyses of transfiction would also allow research in this field to evolve based on comprehensive and robust syntheses, mitigating the risk of repetition of arguments that are by now well-known and tested.

One of the aims of this Element has been to inspire further research in transfiction based on the evidence collected through meta-research. The combination of this meta-analysis and future qualitative meta-analyses may become the starting point for a second generation of transfiction research, following its first thirty years. Unlike the first generation, the characteristics of which have been depicted here, future research may aim specifically to make transfiction materials useful for other areas of Translation Studies, identify and implement novel methodologies to enhance creativity and rigour in this subfield, and foster new collaborative, interdisciplinary, and pedagogical practices.

The methodological possibilities outlined in this section may become fruitful for other relatively 'niche' subfields of Translation Studies that have been characterised by a similar methodological repetition to transfiction, developing a long series of case studies. These may include, but are not limited to, Translator Studies, pseudotranslation, retranslation, self-translation, translation history, and literary translation more generally. Existing case studies in these areas have historically generated hypotheses, as well as challenging existing theories, but comprehensive and systematic studies bringing their conclusions into conversation and condensing the state of the art of each area are still needed. The introduction of meta-analytical research designs into (literary) Translation Studies may gradually break the pattern of focusing on texts in isolation, providing a solid basis from which future research can originate, and new, comprehensive theories and hypotheses can be put forward.

References

Abend-David, Dror, ed. 2019. *Representing Translation: The Representation of Translation and Translators in Contemporary Media*. New York: Bloomsbury.

AIIC 2002. *Workload Study*. Geneva: AIIC. Accessed June 21, 2021. https://aiic.org/document/468/AIICWebzine_FebMar2002_7_AIIC_Interpreter_workload_study_full_report_WLS_Full_Report.pdf.

Anderson, Jean. 2005. 'The double agent: Aspects of literary translator affect as revealed in fictional work by translators'. *Linguistica Antverpiensia* 4 (4): 171–182. https://doi.org/10.52034/lanstts.v4i.134.

Arrojo, Rosemary. 2010. 'Fictional texts as pedagogical tools'. In *Literature in Translation: Teaching Issues and Reading Practices*, edited by Carol Maier and Françoise Massardier-Kenney, 53–68. Kent: The Kent State University Press.

———. 2014. 'The power of fiction as theory: Some exemplary lessons on translation from Borges's stories'. In *Transfiction: Research into the realities of translation fiction*, edited by Klaus Kaindl and Karlheinz Spitzl, 37–49. Amsterdam: John Benjamins.

———. 2018. 'Fictional translators: Rethinking translation through literature'. In *New Perspectives in Translation and Interpreting Studies*, edited by Michael Cronin and Moira Inghilleri. Abingdon: Routledge.

Babel, Reinhard. 2015. *Translationsfiktionen: Zur Hermeneutik, Poetik und Ethik des Übersetzens*. Bielefeld: Transcript Verlag.

Bandia, Paul F., James Hadley, and Siobhán McElduff. 2025. 'Introduction'. In *Translation Classics in Context*, edited by, Paul F. Bandia. James Hadley and Siobhán McElduff, 1–17 Abingdon: Routledge.

Beebee, Thomas O. 2012. *Transmesis: Inside Translation's Black Box*. New York: Palgrave Macmillan.

Ben-Ari, Nitsa. 2010. 'Representations of translators in popular culture'. *Translation and Interpreting Studies* 5 (2): 220–242. https://doi.org/10.1075/tis.5.2.05ben.

———. 2014. 'Reaching a dead-end – and then? Jacques Gélat's *Le Traducteur* and *Le Traducteur amoureux*'. In *Transfiction: Research into the realities of translation fiction*, edited by Klaus Kaindl and Karlheinz Spitzl, 113–123. Amsterdam: John Benjamins.

2021. 'The Translator's Note revisited'. In *Literary Translator Studies*, edited by Klaus Kaindl, Waltraud Kolb and Daniela Schlager, 157–181. Amsterdam: John Benjamins.

Ben-Ari, Nitsa, and Shaul Levin. 2016. 'Translators and (their) authors in the fictional turn'. *Translation and Interpreting Studies* 11 (3): 339–343. https://doi.org/10.1075/tis.11.3.01ben.

Bergantino, Andrea. 2023. 'Translation and its fictions: pseudotranslation and partial cultural translation in focus'. *The Translator* 30 (2): 249–264. https://doi.org/10.1080/13556509.2023.2251892.

2024. 'Translators in Fabula: Bridging Transfiction and Translator Studies through a Comparative Analysis of Contemporary Italian Narratives'. PhD thesis, School of Languages, Literatures and Cultural Studies, Trinity College Dublin.

Bergantino, Andrea, and James Luke Hadley. 2025. 'Human-centredness in Translating with Technology. A Literary Translator Studies meta-analysis'. *InContext. Studies in Translation and Interculturalism* 5 (1): 18–41. https://doi.org/10.54754/incontext.v5i1.111.

Bianciardi, Luciano. 1962/2019. *La vita agra*. Milan: Feltrinelli.

Bocchiola, Massimo. 2015. *Mai più come ti ho visto. Gli occhi del traduttore e il tempo*. Turin: Einaudi.

Borg, Claudine. 2023. 'A literary translation in the making: A process-oriented perspective'. In *Routledge Studies in Literary Translation*, edited by Jacob Blakesley and Duncan Large. New York: Routledge.

Borges, Jorge Luis. 1939/1998. 'Pierre Menard: Author of the *Quixote*'. In *Collected Fictions: Jorge Luis Borges*, Translated by Andrew Hurley, 88–95. New York: Penguin.

Briggs, Kate. 2017/2021. *This Little Art*. 7th ed. London: Fitzcarraldo.

Calleja, Jen. 2023. *Vehicle: A Verse Novel*. London: Prototype.

2024. 'Inhospitable conditions: Hospitality, kinship and complaint in Maureen Freely's *Angry in Piraeus* and Mireille Gansel's *Translation as Transhumance* (tr. Ros Schwartz)'. *Life Writing* 21 (1): 13–32. https://doi.org/10.1080/14484528.2023.2240545.

2025. *Fair: The Life-Art of Translation*. London: Prototype.

Carroll, Noël. 2016. 'Character, social information, and the challenge of psychology'. In *Fictional Characters, Real Problems. The Search for Ethical Content in Literature*, edited by Garry L. Hagberg, 83–101. Oxford: Oxford University Press.

Causadias, José M., Kevin M. Korous, Karina M. Cahill, and Gianna Rea-Sandin. 2023. 'The importance of research about research on culture:

A call for meta-research on culture'. *Cultural Diversity and Ethnic Minority Psychology* 29 (1): 85–95. https://doi.org/10.1037/cdp0000516.

Chesterman, Andrew. 2009. 'The name and nature of translator studies'. *Hermes – Journal of Language and Communication Studies* 42: 13–22.

———. 2016. *Memes of Translation: The Spread of Ideas in Translation Theory*. Revised ed. Amsterdam: John Benjamins.

———. 2021. 'Translator studies'. In *Handbook of Translation Studies*, edited by Yves Gambier and Luc van Doorslaer, 241–246. Amsterdam: John Benjamins.

Cleary, Heather. 2021. 'The translator's visibility. Scenes from contemporary Latin American fiction'. In *Literatures, Cultures, Translation*, edited by Brian James Baer and Michelle Woods. New York: Bloomsbury.

Coppola, Sofia. 2003. *Lost in Translation*. Focus Features.

Croft, Jennifer. 2024. *The Extinction of Irena Rey*. London: Bloomsbury.

Cronin, Michael. 2000. *Across the Lines: Travel, Language, Translation*. Cork: Cork University Press.

———. 2003. *Translation and Globalization*. London: Routledge.

———. 2009. *Translation Goes to the Movies*. Abingdon: Routledge.

———. 2023. 'Translation, ecology, and deep time'. In *Time, Space, Matter in Translation*, edited by Pamela Beattie, Simona Bertacco and Tatjana Soldat-Jaffe, 4–18. Abingdon: Routledge.

Culler, Jonathan. 2010. 'The closeness of close reading'. *ADE Bulletin* 149: 20–25.

Dam, Helle V., and Minna Ruokonen. 2024. 'Bringing in the translators' views on their (in)visibility: The forms and significance of visibility in research on translator status'. In *Beyond the Translator's Invisibility: Critical Reflections and New Perspectives*, edited by Peter J. Freeth and Rafael Treviño, 73–94. Leuven: Leuven University Press.

Dam, Helle V., and Karen Korning Zethsen. 2016. '"I think it is a wonderful job": On the solidity of the translation profession'. *The Journal of Specialised Translation* (25): 174–187.

Delabastita, Dirk. 2009. 'Fictional representations'. In *Routledge Encyclopedia of Translation Studies*, edited by Mona Baker and Gabriela Saldanha, 109–112. Abingdon: Routledge.

———. 2020. 'Fictional representations'. In *Routledge Encyclopedia of Translation Studies*, edited by Mona Baker and Gabriela Saldanha, 189–194. Abingdon: Routledge.

Delabastita, Dirk, and Rainier Grutman. 2005. 'Introduction. Fictional representations of multilingualism and translation'. *Linguistica Antverpiensia* 4: 11–34. https://doi.org/10.52034/lanstts.v4i.

References

Dontcheva-Navratilova, Olga. 2021. 'Engaging with the reader in research articles in English: Variation across disciplines and linguacultural backgrounds'. *English for Specific Purposes* 63: 18–32. https://doi.org/10.1016/j.esp.2021.02.003.

Du, Rui, and Heidi Salaets. 2025. 'Collaborative learning in translation and interpreting: A meta-study'. *The Interpreter and Translator Trainer* 19 (1): 1–26. https://doi.org/10.1080/1750399X.2025.2453356.

Eakin, Paul. 2020. 'Writing life writing: Narrative, history, autobiography'. In *Routledge Auto/Biography Studies*, edited by Ricia A. Chansky. New York: Routledge.

Eberharter, Markus. 2021. 'Translator biographies as a contribution to Translator Studies: Case studies from nineteenth-century Galicia'. In *Literary Translator Studies*, edited by Klaus Kaindl, Waltraud Kolb and Daniela Schlager, 73–88. Amsterdam: John Benjamins.

Ferrante, Elena. 2013. *Storia di chi fugge e di chi resta*. Rome: Edizioni e/o.

2014. *Storia della bambina perduta*. Rome: Edizioni e/o.

Flick, Uwe. 2022. 'Revitalising triangulation for designing multi-perspective qualitative research'. In *The SAGE Handbook of Qualitative Research Design*, edited by Uwe Flick, 652–664. London: SAGE.

Flyvbjerg, Bent. 2006. 'Five misunderstandings about case-study research'. *Qualitative Inquiry* 12 (2): 219–245. https://doi.org/10.1177/1077800405284363.

Freeth, Peter. 2024. 'Introduction'. In *Beyond the Translator's Invisibility: Critical Reflections and New Perspectives*, edited by Peter Freeth and Rafael Treviño, 7–28. Leuven: Leuven University Press.

Friel, Brian. 1980/2012. *Translations*. London: Faber and Faber.

Gambier, Yves. 2018. 'Institutionalization of translation studies'. In *A History of Modern Translation Knowledge. Sources, Concepts, Effects*, edited by Lieven D'hulst and Yves Gambier, 179–194. Amsterdam: John Benjamins.

2023. 'The conceptualisation of translation in translation studies: A response'. *Translation Studies* 16 (2): 317–322. https://doi.org/10.1080/14781700.2023.2209576.

Gentes, Eva, and Trish Van and Bolderen. 2022. 'Self-Translation'. In *The Routledge Handbook of Literary Translingualism*, edited by Steven G. Kellman and Natasha Lvovich, 369–381. New York: Routledge.

Gentzler, Edwin. 2008. *Translation and Identity in the Americas: New Directions in Translation Theory*. Abingdon: Routledge.

Giraldo, Juan G. Ramírez, and Laura E. V. Piracón. 2023. '"Scrambled tongues united in a single voice": Transfiction in contemporary Colombian literature'. In *Transfiction and Bordering Approaches to Theorizing Translation. Essays in Dialogue with the Work of Rosemary Arrojo*, edited by D. M. Spitzer and Paulo Oliveira, 111–124. New York: Routledge.

Godbout, Patricia. 2014. 'Fictional translators in Québec novels'. In *Transfiction: Research into the Realities of Translation Fiction*, edited by Klaus Kaindl and Karlheinz Spitzl, 177–187. Amsterdam: John Benjamins.

Grass, Delphine. 2023. *Translation as Creative–Critical Practice*. Cambridge: Cambridge University Press.

Grass, Delphine, and Lily Robert-Foley. 2024. 'The translation memoir: An introduction'. *Life Writing* 21 (1): 1–9. https://doi.org/10.1080/14484528.2023.2281044.

Güércio, Nayara. 2025. 'Mapping indirect translation research: A two-tier meta-analysis of traditions, shifts, and uncharted paths'. PhD thesis, School of Languages, Literatures and Cultural Studies, Trinity College Dublin.

Hadley, James, and Motoko Akashi. 2015. 'Translation and celebrity: The translation strategies of Haruki Murakami and their implications for the visibility paradigm'. *Perspectives: Studies in Translation Theory and Practice* 23 (3): 458–474. https://doi.org/10.1080/0907676X.2014.998688.

Hadley, James Luke. 2023. *Systematically Analysing Indirect Translations: Putting the Concatenation Effect Hypothesis to the Test*, Routledge Advances in Translation and Interpreting Studies. New York: Routledge.

Hagedorn, Hans Christian. 2006. *La traducción narrada: el recurso narrativo de la traducción ficticia*. Cuenca: Ediciones de la Universidad de Castilla – La Mancha.

Hahn, Daniel. 2022. *Catching Fire: A Translation Diary*. Edinburgh: Charco Press.

Heino, Anu. 2020. 'Finnish literary translators and the Illusio of the field'. In *New Horizons in Translation Research and Education 5*, edited by Anne Ketola, Tamara Mikolič Južnič, and Outi Paloposki, 141–157. Tampere: Tampere University. http://urn.fi/URN:ISBN:978-952-03-1585-6.

Hermans, Theo. 2022. *Translation and History: A Textbook*. Abingdon: Routledge.

Herrnstein Smith, Barbara. 2016. 'What was "close reading"? A century of method in literary studies'. *Minnesota Review* 87: 57–75.

Holmes, James S. 1972/2000. 'The name and nature of translation studies'. In *The Translation Studies Reader*, edited by Lawrence Venuti, 172–185. London: Routledge.

Hoon, Christina. 2013. 'Meta-synthesis of qualitative case studies: An approach to theory building'. *Organizational Research Methods* 16 (4): 522–556. https://doi.org/10.1177/1094428113484969.

Huang, Qin, and Furong Liu. 2019. 'International translation studies from 2014 to 2018: A bibliometric analysis and its implications'. *Translation Review* 105 (1): 34–57. https://doi.org/10.1080/07374836.2019.1664959.

Hyland, Ken. 2001. 'Brining in the reader: Addressee features in academic articles'. *Written Communication* 18 (4): 549–574. https://doi.org/10.1177/074108830101800.

Ioannidis, John P. A. 2024. 'What meta-research has taught us about research and changes to research practices'. *Journal of Economic Surveys* 39, 1–12. https://doi.org/10.1111/joes.12666.

Ivancic, Barbara. 2022. 'Diamo spazio ai Translator Studies: il traduttore letterario come soggetto e oggetto di studio'. In *Lezioni di traduzione*, edited by Alberto Alberti and Nadzieja Bąkowska, 105–122. Bologna: LILEC.

Ivančić, Barbara, and Alexandra L. Zepter. 2021. 'On the bodily dimension of translators and translating'. In *Genetic Translation Studies. Conflict and Collaboration in Liminal Spaces*, edited by Ariadne Nunes, Joana Moura and Marta Pacheco Pinto, 123–134. London: Bloomsbury.

John, Eileen. 2016. 'Caring about characters'. In *Fictional Characters, Real Problems. The Search for Ethical Content in Literature*, edited by Garry L. Hagberg, 31–46. Oxford: Oxford University Press.

Kaindl, Klaus. 2012. 'Representation of translators and interpreters'. In *Handbook of Translation Studies*, edited by Yves Gambier and Luc van Doorslaer, 145–150. Amsterdam: John Benjamins.

2014. 'Going fictional! Translators and interpreters in literature and film. An introduction'. In *Transfiction: Research into the Realities of Translation Fiction*, edited by Klaus Kaindl and Karlheinz Spitzl, 1–26. Amsterdam: John Benjamins.

2016. 'Fictional representations of translators and interpreters'. In *Researching Translation and Interpreting*, edited by Claudia V. Angelelli and Brian James Baer, 71–82. London: Routledge.

2018a. 'Fictional representations'. In *A History of Modern Translation Knowledge*, edited by Lieven D'hulst and Yves Gambier, 51–56. Amsterdam: John Benjamins.

2018b. 'The remaking of the translator's reality: The role of fiction in translation studies'. In *The Fictions of Translation*, edited by Judith Woodsworth, 157–170. Amsterdam: John Benjamins.

2021. '(Literary) Translator Studies. Shaping the field'. In *Literary Translator Studies*, edited by Klaus Kaindl, Waltraud Kolb and Daniela Schlager, 1–38. Amsterdam: John Benjamins.

2023. 'The centrality of the margins: The translator's footnote as *Parergon*'. In *Transfiction and Bordering Approaches to Theorizing Translation: Essays in Dialogue with the Work of Rosemary Arrojo*, edited by D. M. Spitzer and Paulo Oliveira, 25–40. New York: Routledge.

2025. 'The translator's nested identities: Translator studies and the auto/biographical turn'. *Perspectives: Studies in Translation Theory and Practice* 33, 326–340. https://doi.org/10.1080/0907676X.2024.2421772.

Kaindl, Klaus, Waltraud Kolb, and Daniela Schlager, eds. 2021. 'Literary translator studies'. In *Benjamins Translation Library*, edited by Roberto A. Valdeón. Vol. 156, Amsterdam: John Benjamins.

Kaindl, Klaus, and Ingrid Kurz, eds. 2005. *Wortklauber, Sinnverdreher, Brückenbauer: ÜbersetzerInnen und DolmetscherInnen als literarischer Geschöpfe*. Vol. 1, *Im Spiegel der Literatur*. Vienna: Lit Verlag.

eds. 2008. *Helfer, Verräter, Gaukler? Das Rollenbild von TranslatorInnen im Spiegel der Literatur*. Vol. 3, *Im Spiegel der Literatur*. Berlin: Lit Verlag.

2010a. 'Einleitung'. In *Machtlos, selbstlos, meinunglos? Interdisziplinäre Analysen von ÜbersetzerInnen und DolmetscherInnen in belletristischen Werken*, edited by Klaus Kaindl and Ingrid Kurz, 9–16. Berlin: Lit Verlag.

eds. 2010b. *Machtlos, selbstlos, meinunglos? Interdisziplinäre Analysen von ÜbersetzerInnen und DolmetscherInnen in belletristischen Werken*. Vol. 5, *Im Spiegel der Literatur*. Vienna: Lit Verlag.

Kaindl, Klaus, and Karlheinz Spitzl, eds. 2014. 'Transfiction: Research into the realities of translation fiction'. In *Benjamins Translation Library*, edited by Yves Gambier. Vol. 110, Amsterdam: John Benjamins.

Klarer, Mario. 2004. *An Introduction to Literary Studies*. 2nd ed., London: Routledge.

Kolb, Waltraud, Sonja Pöllabauer, and Mira Kadrić. 2024. '"Von den Rändern ins Zentrum." Die Wissenschatsreise von Klaus Kaindl'. In *Translation als Gestaltung: Beiträge für Klaus Kaindl zur translatorischen Theorie und Praxis*, edited by Mira Kadric, Waltraud Kolb and Sonja Pöllabauer, 11–20. Tübingen: Narr Francke Attempto.

Kripper, Denise. 2023. 'Narratives of mistranslation: Fictional translators in Latin American literature'. In *Routledge Studies in Literary Translation*, edited by Jacob Blakesley and Duncan Large. New York: Routledge.

Kuang, Rebecca F. 2022. *Babel or the Necessity of Violence: An Arcane History of the Oxford Translators' Revolution*. New York: Harper Collins.

Kupsch-Losereit, Sigrid. 2014. 'Pseudotranslations in 18th century France'. In *Transfiction: Research into the Realities of Translation Fiction*, edited by Klaus Kaindl and Karlheinz Spitzl, 189–200. Amsterdam: John Benjamins.

Lahiri, Jhumpa. 2015. *In Altre Parole*. Milan: Guanda.

2016. *In Other Words*. Translated by Ann Goldstein. London: Bloomsbury.

Lakhous, Amara. 2006/2011. *Scontro di civiltà per un ascensore a piazza Vittorio*. Rome: Edizioni e/o.

Lavieri, Antonio. 2007/2016. *Translatio in fabula. La letteratura come pratica teorica del tradurre*. Rome: Editori Riuniti.

Lenart-Cheng, Helga, and Ioana Luca. 2025. 'Life writing and world literature: Introduction'. In *Life Writing as World Literature*, edited by Helga Lenart-Cheng and Ioana Luca, 1–16. New York: Bloomsbury.

Levi-Strauss, Claude. 1966. *The Savage Mind*. Translated by N. N. Chicago: University of Chicago Press.

López, Belén Santana, and Críspulo Travieso Rodríguez. 2021. 'Staging the literary translator in bibliographic catalogs'. In *Literary Translator Studies*, edited by Klaus Kaindl, Waltraud Kolb and Daniela Schlager, 89–104. Amsterdam: John Benjamins.

Lowe, Derek. 2015. 'Seeing through the 'Burden of the Past': Superior Belatedness in Keats's "On First Looking into Chapman's Homer"'. *The Keats-Shelley Review* 29 (2): 105–116. https://doi.org/10.1179/0952414215Z.00000000060.

Lowney, Declan. 1996. 'Father Ted'. In *Rock a Hula Ted*.

Maher, Brigid. 2019. 'Pseudotranslation'. In *The Routledge Handbook of Literary Translation*, edited by Kelly Washbourne and Ben Van Wyke, 382–393. Oxford: Routledge.

Maier, Carol. 2014. 'The translator as theôros: Thoughts on cogitation, figuration and current creative writing'. In *Translating Others*, edited by Theo Hermans, 163–180. Abingdon: Routledge.

Marin-Lacarta, Maialen, and Chuan Yu. 2023. 'Ethnographic research in translation and interpreting studies'. *The Translator* 29 (2): 147–156. https://doi.org/10.1080/13556509.2023.2233291.

McDonough Dolmaya, Julie. 2024. 'Digital research methods for translation studies'. In *Research Methods in Translation and Interpreting Studies*, edited by Callum Walker and Federico M. Federici. Aingdon: Routledge.

Meister, Lova. 2018. 'On methodology: How mixed methods research can contribute to translation studies'. *Translation Studies* 11 (1): 66–83. https://doi.org/10.1080/14781700.2017.1374206.

Mellinger, Christopher D., and Thomas A. Hanson. 2021. 'Methodological considerations for survey research: Validity, reliability, and quantitative analysis'. *Linguistica Antverpiensia* 19: 172–190. https://doi.org/10.52034/lanstts.v19i0.549.

Miletich, Marko. 2024a. 'Introduction'. In *Transfiction: Characters in Search of Translation Studies*, edited by Marko Miletich, xv–xxiii. Wilmington: Vernon Press.

——— ed. 2024b. *Transfiction: Characters in Search of Translation Studies*, Series in Literary Studies. Wilmington: Vernon Press.

Milkova, Stiliana. 2022. *Storia delle prime volte*. Rome: Voland.

Mossop, Brian. 1996. 'The image of translation in science fiction and astronomy'. *The Translator* 2 (1): 1–26.

——— 2023. 'Translation and architecturally odd invented languages in science fiction'. *Translation Studies* 17 (2): 265–281. https://doi.org/10.1080/14781700.2023.2261943.

Munday, Jeremy. 2014. 'Using primary sources to produce a microhistory of translation and translators: Theoretical and methodological concerns'. *The Translator* 20 (1): 64–80. https://doi.org/10.1080/13556509.2014.899094.

Munday, Jeremy, Sara Ramos Pinto, and Jacob Blakesley. 2022. *Introducing Translation Studies. Theories and Applications*. fifth ed. Abingdon: Routledge.

Murakami, Haruki. 2015. *Wind/Pinball: Two Novels*. Translated by Ted Goossen. New York: Knopf.

NíGhríofa, Doireann. 2020. *A Ghost in the Throat*. Dublin: Tramp Press.

Nunes, Ariadne, Joana Moura, and Marta Pacheco Pinto. 2021. 'What is genetic translation studies good for?' In *Genetic Translation Studies: Conflict and Collaboration in Liminal Spaces*, edited by Ariadne Nunes, Joana Moura and Marta Pacheco Pinto, 1–23. London: Bloomsbury.

Ohrvik, Ane. 2024. 'What is close reading? An exploration of a methodology'. *Rethinking History: The Journal of Theory and Practice* 28 (2): 238–260. https://doi.org/10.1080/13642529.2024.2345001.

Olalla-Soler, Christian, Javier Franco Aixelá, and Sara Rovira-Esteva. 2022. 'Fifty years of hectic history in translation studies'. In *50 Years Later: What Have We Learnt after Holmes (1972) and Where Are We Now?*, edited by Javier Franco Aixelá and Christian Olalla-Soler, 15–40. Las Palmas de Gran Canaria: Universidad de Las Palmas de Gran Canaria. Servicio de Publicaciones y Difusión Científica.

Pagano, Adriana S. 2002. 'Translation as testimony: On official histories and subversive pedagogies in Cortázar'. In *Translation and Power*, edited by

Maria Tymoczko and Edwin Gentzler, 80–98. Amherst: University of Massachusetts Press.

Polezzi, Loredana. 2012. 'Translation and migration'. *Translation Studies* 5 (3): 345–356. https://doi.org/10.1080/14781700.2012.701943.

Pym, Anthony. 2009. 'Humanizing translation history'. *Hermes – Journal of Language and Communication Studies* 42: 23–48. https://doi.org/10.7146/hjlcb.v22i42.96845.

Querido, Alessandra Matias. 2011. 'Investigando Jerônimos: A rapresentaçâo do tradutor como personagem em narrativas contemporâneas'. PhD thesis, Departamento de Teoria Literária e Literaturas, Universidade de Brasília.

Rath, Brigitte. 2024. 'Pseudotranslation'. In *Translation and the Classic*, edited by Paul F. Bandia, James Luke Hadley and Siobhán McElduff, 111–138. Abingdon: Routledge.

Rebora, Simone. 2023. 'Sentiment analysis in literary studies. A Critical Survey'. *DHQ: Digital Humanities Quarterly* 17 (2). https://dhq.digitalhumanities.org/vol/17/2/000691/000691.html.

Rigney, Ann. 2019. 'Texts and intertextuality'. In *The Life of Texts: An Introduction to Literary Studies*, edited by Kiene Brillenburg Wurth and Ann Rigney, 79–111. Amsterdam: Amsterdam University Press.

Risku, Hanna. 2024. 'Reflections on individualized and extended translator studies'. In *Translation als Gestaltung: Beiträge für Klaus Kaindl zur translatorischen Theorie und Praxis*, edited by Mira Kadric, Waltraud Kolb and Sonja Pöllabauer, 65–74. Tübingen: Narr Francke Attempto.

Robinson, Douglas. 1991. *The Translator's Turn*. Baltimore: John Hopkins University Press.

Rosenwald, Lawrence. 2016. 'Reflections on translators and authors: Autobiographical, polemical, historical'. *Translation and Interpreting Studies* 11 (3): 344–360. https://doi.org/10.1075/tis.11.3.02ros.

Rossari, Marco. 2023. *L'ombra del vulcano*. Turin: Einaudi.

Rovira-Esteva, Sara, Javier Franco Aixelá, and Christian Olalla-Soler. 2019. 'Citation patterns in translation studies: A format-dependent bibliometric analysis'. *Translation & Interpreting* 11 (1): 147–171. https://doi.org/10.12807/ti.111201.2019.a09.

Ruffo, Paola. 2022. 'Collecting literary translators' narratives: Towards a new paradigm for technological innovation in literary translation'. In *Using Technologies for Creative-Text Translation*, edited by James Luke Hadley, Kristiina Taivalkoski-Shilov, Carlos S. C. Teixeira and Antonio Toral, 18–39. New York: Routledge.

Ruokonen, Minna, Elin Svahn, and Anu Heino. 2024. 'Translators' and interpreters' job satisfaction – a multi-faceted object of study with far-reaching implications'. *Translation Spaces* 13 (1): 1–6. https://doi.org/10.1075/ts.00032.ruo.

Ruokonen, Minna, Jannika Lassus, and Taru Virtanen. 2020. "'I fulfil my place among the humankind, in the universe': Finnish translators' job satisfaction in three empirical studies'. *MikaEL* 13: 109–123. https://www.sktl.fi/liitto/seminaarit/mikael-verkkojulkaisu/vol/mikael-vol13-2020/.

Saldanha, Gabriela, and Sharon O'Brien. 2013. *Research Methodologies in Translation Studies*. Abingdon: Routledge.

Schoeneborn, Dennis, and Joep Cornelissen. 2022. 'Fictional inquiry'. In *Handbook of Philosophy of Management*, edited by Cristina Neesham, Markus Reihlen and Dennis Schoeneborn, 139–158. Cham: Springer.

Sela-Sheffy, Rakefet. 2005. 'How to be a (recognized) translator: Rethinking habitus, norms, and the field of translation'. *Target. International Journal of Translation Studies* 17 (1): 1–26. https://doi.org/10.1075/target.17.1.02sel.

Sepp, Arvi. 2018. 'Moving texts: The representation of the translator in Yoko Tawada's and Emine Sevgi Özdamar's stories'. In *The Fictions of Translation*, edited by Judith Woodsworth, 139–153. Amsterdam: John Benjamins.

Spitzer, D. M. 2017. 'Past the fire's edge: Figures of translation from Herodotos 1.86'. *Translation Review* 99 (1): 15–25. https://doi.org/10.1080/07374836.2017.1359128.

Spitzer, David M., and Paulo Oliveira, eds. 2023. *Transfiction and Bordering Approaches to Theorizing Translation*: Essays in Dialogue with the Work of Rosemary Arrojo, Routledge Advances in Translation and Interpreting Studies. New York: Routledge.

Spitzer, David M. 2023. 'Introduction: Bordering approaches & trans-bordering themes in dialogue with the work of Rosemary Arrojo'. In *Transfiction and Bordering Approaches to Theorizing Translation: Essays in Dialogue with the Work of Rosemary Arrojo*, edited by D. M. Spitzer and Paulo Oliveira, 1–17. New York: Routledge.

Spitzl, Karlheinz. 2014. 'Fiction as a catalyst. Some afterthoughts'. In *Transfiction: Research into the Realities of Translation Fiction*, edited by Klaus Kaindl and Karlheinz Spitzl, 363–368. Amsterdam: John Benjamins.

Sternberg, Meir. 1981. 'Polylingualism as reality and translation as mimesis'. *Poetics Today* 2 (4): 221–239.

Strümper-Krobb, Sabine. 2003. 'The translator in fiction'. *Intercultural Communication* 3 (2): 115–121. https://doi.org/10.1080/14708470308668095.

2009. *Zwischen den Welten: Die Sichtbarkeit des Übersetzers in der Literatur*. Berlin: WEIDLER.

2013. '"A good metaphor for all we do?" Fictional translators as criminals and detectives: Some examples'. In *Translation Right or Wrong*, edited by Susana Bayó Belenguer, Eiléan Ní Chuilleanáin and Cormac Ó Cuilleanáin, 130–139. Dublin: Four Courts Press.

2018. 'Pretending not to be original: Pseudotranslations and their functions'. In *The Fictions of Translation*, edited by Judith Woodsworth, 199–213. Amsterdam: John Benjamins.

2021. 'George Egerton and Eleanor Marx as mediators of Scandinavian literature'. In *Literary Translator Studies*, edited by Klaus Kaindl, Waltraud Kolb and Daniela Schlager, 55–71. Amsterdam: John Benjamins.

2022. 'The translator's visibility: Scenes from contemporary Latin American fiction'. *Translation Studies* 15 (3): 343–346. https://doi.org/10.1080/14781700.2022.2032308.

Susam-Sarajeva, Şebnem. 2009. 'The case study research method in translation studies'. *The Interpreter and Translator Trainer* 3 (1): 37–56. https://doi.org/10.1080/1750399X.2009.10798780.

Svahn, Elin. 2020. 'The dynamics of extratextual translatorship in contemporary Sweden. A mixed methods approach'. PhD thesis, Stockholm University. Urn:nbn:se:su:diva-177365.

Thiem, Jon. 1995. 'The translator as hero in postmodern fiction'. *Translation and Literature* 4 (2): 207–218.

Tight, Malcolm. 2017. *Understanding Case Study Research: Small-scale Research with Meaning*. London: SAGE.

Timulak, Ladislav, and Mary Creaner. 2022. 'Meta-analysis in qualitative research: A descriptive-interpretative approach'. In *The SAGE Handbook of Qualitative Research Design*, edited by Uwe Flick, 555–570. London: SAGE.

Todorova, Marija. 2014. 'Interpreting conflict: Memories of an interpreter'. In *Transfiction. Research into the Realities of Translation Fiction*, edited by Klaus Kaindl and Karlheinz Spitzl, 221–231. Amsterdam: John Benjamins.

Valdeón, Roberto A. 2011. 'On fictional turns, fictionalizing twists and the invention of the Americas'. *Translation and Interpreting Studies* 6 (2): 207–224. https://doi.org/10.1075/tis.6.2.06val.

Venuti, Lawrence, ed. 2012. *The Translation Studies Reader*. 3rd ed. Abingdon: Routledge.

2019. *Contra Instrumentalism: A Translation Polemic*. Edited by Marco Abel and Roland Végső, *Provocations*. Lincoln: University of Nebraska Press.

Vieira, Else. 1995. '(In)visibilidades na tradução: Troca de olhares teóricos e ficcionais'. *ComTextos* 6:50–68.

Villeneuve, Denis. 2016. *Arrival*. United States: Paramount Pictures.

Wakabayashi, Judy. 2011. 'Fictional representations of author–translator relationships'. *Translation Studies* 4 (1): 87–102. https://doi.org/10.1080/14781700.2011.528684.

Wilhelm, Christine. 2010. *Traduttore traditore – Vermittler durch Verrat. Eine Analyse literarischer Translatorfiguren in Texten von Jorge Luis Borges, Italo Calvino und Leonardo Sciascia*. Vol. 46, *Literatur, Imagination, Realität*. Trier: Wissenschaftlicher Verlag Trier.

Wilson, Rita. 2007. 'The fiction of the translator'. *Journal of Intercultural Studies* 28 (4): 381–395. https://doi.org/10.1080/07256860701591219.

2009. 'The writer's double: Translation, writing, and autobiography'. *Romance Studies* 27 (3): 186–198. https://doi.org/10.1179/174581509X455150.

Woodsworth, Judith, ed. 2018. 'The fictions of translation'. In *Benjamins Translation Library*, edited by Roberto A. Valdeón. Vol. 139. Amsterdam: John Benjamins.

2021. 'Dressing up for Halloween: Walking the line between translating and writing'. In *Literary Translator Studies*, edited by Klaus Kaindl, Waltraud Kolb and Daniela Schlager, 293–306. Amsterdam: John Benjamins.

Woodsworth, Judith, and Gillian Lane-Mercier. 2018. 'Introduction: Translation as a master metaphor'. In *The Fictions of Translation*, edited by Judith Woodsworth, 1–12. Amsterdam: John Benjamins.

Wozniak, Monika. 2014. 'Future imperfect: Translation and translators in science-fiction novels and films'. In *Transfiction: Research into the Realities of Translation Fiction*, edited by Klaus Kaindl and Karlheinz Spitzl, 345–361. Amsterdam: John Benjamins.

Xhoga, Ledia. 2025. *Misinterpretation*. London: Daunt Books.

Youdale, Roy. 2020. *Using Computers in the Translation of Literary Style: Challenges and Opportunities, Routledge Advances in Translation and Interpreting Studies*. New York: Routledge.

Acknowledgements

My sincere gratitude goes to all the inspiring colleagues I have met at the Trinity Centre for Literary and Cultural Translation, where I completed this project. In particular, I would like to thank James Hadley and Nayara Güércio for encouraging me to think in different ways, as well as for being exceptional mentors, colleagues, and friends.

Cambridge Elements =

Translation and Interpreting

The series is edited by Kirsten Malmkjær with Sabine Braun as associate editor for Elements focusing on Interpreting.

Kirsten Malmkjær
University of Leicester

Kirsten Malmkjær is Professor Emeritus of Translation Studies at the University of Leicester. She has taught Translation Studies at the universities of Birmingham, Cambridge, Middlesex and Leicester and has written extensively on aspects of both the theory and practice of the discipline. *Translation and Creativity* (London: Routledge) was published in 2020 and *The Cambridge Handbook of Translation*, which she edited, was published in 2022. She is preparing a volume entitled *Introducing Translation* for the Cambridge Introductions to Language and Linguistics series.

Editorial Board

Adriana Serban, *Université Paul Valéry*
Barbara Ahrens, *Technische Hochschule Köln*
Liu Min-Hua, *Hong Kong Baptist University*
Christine Ji, *The University of Sydney*
Jieun Lee, *Ewha Womans University*
Lorraine Leeson, *The University of Dublin*
Sara Laviosa, *Università degli Studi di Bari Aldo Moro*
Fabio Alves, *FALE-UFMG*
Moira Inghilleri, *University of Massachusetts Amherst*
Akiko Sakamoto, *University of Portsmouth*
Haidee Kotze, *Utrecht University*

About the Series

Elements in Translation and Interpreting present cutting edge studies on the theory, practice and pedagogy of translation and interpreting. The series also features work on machine learning and AI, and human-machine interaction, exploring how they relate to multilingual societies with varying communication and accessibility needs, as well as text-focused research.

Cambridge Elements

Translation and Interpreting

Elements in the Series

Translation as Creative–Critical Practice
Delphine Grass

Translation in Analytic Philosophy
Francesca Ervas

Towards Game Translation User Research
Mikołaj Deckert, Krzysztof W. Hejduk, and Miguel Á. Bernal-Merino

An Extraordinary Chinese Translation of Holocaust Testimony
Meiyuan Zhao

Hypertranslation
Mª Carmen África Vidal Claramonte and Tong King Lee

Researching and Modelling the Translation Process
Muhammad M. M. Abdel Latif

Risk Management in Translation
Anthony Pym

Literary Exophonic Translation
Lúcia Collischonn

Translating His-stories
Mª Carmen África Vidal Claramonte

Charting Translation Reception: Methods and Challenges
Bei Hu

A Zombie Theory of Translation: Or, What is a "Revenant" Translation?
Douglas Robinson

Charting Transfiction: Patterns, Open Questions, and Future Directions
Andrea Bergantino

A full series listing is available at: www.cambridge.org/EITI

For EU product safety concerns, contact us at Calle de José Abascal, 56–1°,
28003 Madrid, Spain or eugpsr@cambridge.org.

www.ingramcontent.com/pod-product-compliance
Lightning Source LLC
LaVergne TN
LVHW011856060526
838200LV00054B/4356